Devils Tower

Stories in Stone

D0096687

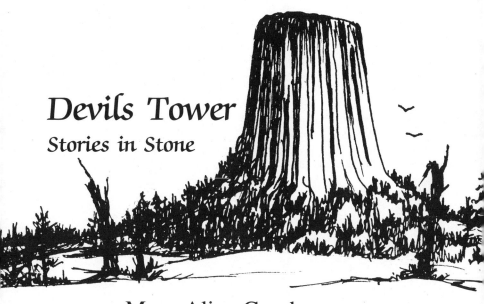

Devils Tower
Stories in Stone

Mary Alice Gunderson

With a foreword by

Raymond J. DeMallie

HIGH PLAINS PRESS
Glendo, Wyoming

Both the epigraph and the Kiowa legend of Devils Tower are from N. Scott Momaday's *The Way to Rainy Mountain* (University of New Mexico Press, copyright 1969) and are reprinted with permission of the publisher.

The Indian pictograph of the Black Hills is from *A Pictographic History of the Oglala Sioux*, by Amos Bad Heart Bull, text by Helen Blish, by permission of the University of Nebraska Press. Copyright © 1967 by the University of Nebraska Press.

The cover painting, "Spring Renewal," is by Gisele Robinson of Devils Tower, Wyoming.

Library of Congress Cataloging in Publication Data
Gunderson, Mary Alice, 1936–
Devils Tower : stories in stone /
Mary Alice Gunderson
with a foreword by Raymond J. DeMallie.
p. cm.
Bibliography: p
Includes index.
1. Devils Tower National Monument (Wyo.)—History.
I. Title
F767D47G86 1988   88-16492
978.7'13—dc19   CIP
ISBN 0-931271-09-6 (pbk.)

*For my husband and my son
and in memory of my father*

Foreword

In the vast, rolling expanses of the Great Plains, the badlands, hills, buttes and mountains take on special grandeur and awesomeness. To the American Indian peoples who are the aboriginal inhabitants of this land, these places—out of the ordinary, singled out by their uniqueness—are especially sacred, places where humankind comes face to face with the powers beyond knowing. Especially is this true of the Black Hills and the two great isolated buttes that guard them on the northeast and northwest, Bear Butte and Devils Tower. Remarkable as geological phenomena, they are at the same time enduring connections to another mode of experiencing the world and its natural beauty—a native American way.

More than a century ago, Edwin Denig, long-time fur trader on the Upper Missouri River, recorded the Sioux belief that the billows of smoke and rumblings of thunder emanating from the fastness of the Black Hills were the breath of the "Big White Man" trapped beneath Thunder Mountain in "punishment for being the first aggressor in their territory." Denig wrote: "They say that he issues forth on occasion and his tracks seen in the snow are twenty feet in length. He is condemned to perpetual incarceration under the mountain as an example to all whites to leave the Indians in quiet possession of their hunting ground."[1] But in time the white men came to possess the Black Hills; no wonder today the thunder is heard no longer. Yet the symbol is a powerful one still. No other place is so special to the Sioux, and many still long for the Hills to be returned to the Indian people.

After the turn of this century, an Oglala Sioux warrior-artist named Bad Heart Bull drew a remarkable schematic map (pp. 42–44) of the Black Hills in whose place names and mythological allusions worlds of ancient meaning can be glimpsed, though not fully understood.[2] This map locates Devils Tower in the middle of the Black Hills, to the north of center—a geographical inaccuracy, but reflecting Sioux perception of the central position of the butte. Bad Heart Bull labels it *Mato tipi paha*, meaning "Bear lodge hill," and his drawing depicts it as distinctly phallic in outline. In the 1930s, the Sioux linguist Ella Deloria learned that one of the old Sioux names for the butte was *Wicace paha*, "human penis hill," but she did not learn the significance of the name, or any tale to explicate its origin.[3] Perhaps the shape of the butte suggested its generative power, lying in the heart of the country claimed by the Sioux.

Everyone sees in Devils Tower what expectation and cultural values dictate. The first white Americans to view it perceived it as, in the words of geologist Henry Newton, "an unfailing object of wonder," a tower, resembling the unfinished base of the Washington Monument that stood through many years of the nineteenth

---

[1]Edwin Thompson Denig, *Five Indian Tribes of the Upper Missouri*, edited by John C. Ewers (Norman: University of Oklahoma Press, 1961), p. 6.

[2]Amos Bad Heart Bull, *A Pictographic History of the Oglala Sioux* (Lincoln: University of Nebraska Press, 1967), p. 289.

[3]Personal correspondence, Ella Deloria to John P. Harrington, May 28, 1938 (National Anthropological Archives, Smithsonian Institution, MS. no. 6070).

century as a prominent landmark of the capital city. And, more in the spirit of the place, they thought of it as resembling an Indian tipi.[4]

On early maps the tower was called Bear Lodge, borrowing a name applied by the Sioux and many other tribes. In mundane explanation, the name referred to the large number of bears that lived in the wooded area surrounding the butte. But more symbolic significance applies to the great she-bear of mythology, who scratched at the sides of the butte, scoring it for eternity, as it rose into the sky, carrying a group of children to safety. The soaring height of the tower inevitably makes it, in human perception, a link between earth and sky. For Sioux people—and for other native peoples of the Plains—the eight stars of the constellation Gemini, envisioned as a circle, are called Bear Lodge, and we can assume that these are the children carried skyward to escape their crazed bear-sister.[5]

Exactly how the name Devils Tower, or Bad God's Tower, originated is no longer known. Although Newton attributed to it an American Indian origin, no specific tribe is indicated. It seems more likely to be a white man's designation, for it connotes an evil spirit that has no counterpart in Plains Indian cultures. Like so many place names everywhere, its true origin and significance are irretrievably lost.

As we experience and contemplate Devils Tower—still, even in the modern age, ''an unfailing object of wonder''—each of us must create for it our own private meaning. By bringing

---

[4]Henry Newton and Walter P. Jenney, *Report on the Geology and Resources of the Black Hills of Dakota* (Washington: Government Printing Office, 1880), p. 201; W. F. Raynolds, *Report to the Secretary of War . . . on the exploration of the Yellowstone and the country drained by that river . . .* (40th Congress, 1st session, Senate Executive Document 77, serial set no. 1317, Washington: Government Printing Office, 1868), p. 32.

[5]Eugene Buechel, S.J., *A Dictionary of the Teton Dakota Sioux Language*, edited by Paul Manhart, S.J. (Pine Ridge, S. Dak.: Red Cloud Indian School, 1970), p. 334.

together in these pages the stories of native peoples and new-comers alike, Mary Alice Gunderson has provided a richness of historical depth and cultural diversity that helps us shape our perception of the grandeur of the place, situating personal experience in the perspective of those who came here before us. In that sense, too, Devils Tower is a powerful link, not only between earth and sky, but between present and past.

RAYMOND J. DEMALLIE
Professor of Anthropology
Indiana University, Bloomington

Preface

Somewhere I read that a book is a journey. This one, then, began some years ago on a family trip to Devils Tower National Monument when we shared for the first time this unique place with our young son. He was delighted and overwhelmed. We saw it new, through his eyes.

The tower had always seemed much more than a geologic wonder formed by wind and weather, rising from a beautiful valley. To me it was a place of great mystery, where spiritual strength as well as peace flowed outward from the earth. I wanted to know more about it: its importance to settlers and explorers, to the first climbers to stand on its summit, and, in particular, its importance to American Indian people. What names did they know it by? Were there other legends besides the few I had read?

A generous grant, in 1980, from the Wyoming Council for the Humanities, made funds available for research. I developed an initial history, from which this book is adapted.

Over a period of several years—many times as a family of three —we traveled to Indian reservations, library conventions and Plains Indian conferences to interview individuals and talk with anthropologists. I rediscovered many books and borrowed a number through inter-library loan. We searched archives for articles, scientific dissertations, government documents, newspaper clipping files and microfilm. We dug in dusty state newspaper morgues. I interviewed people in person, by mail and by phone. Some individuals unable to directly assist me supplied phone numbers and addresses of those who could. Several went out of their way to borrow rare documents and photos and hand-carry them to me. Once a computer from the National Archives returned my call, and a metallic voice instructed me to stand by for further information.

Among the things we learned was that the tower's official name is Devils Tower and not "Devil's Tower." The apostrophe was omitted from the original Congressional bill designating it our nation's first national monument, and the omission has continued because of the amount of paperwork involved in changing it.

Also, I learned that a book is the product of many minds and many hands.

Numerous people helped me to locate source materials, in particular Emmet D. Chisum, Research Historian at the Western History Research Center, University of Wyoming. I am especially grateful for the help from the staff at Goodstein Foundation Library, Casper College, which has never let me down. I am also appreciative of the staff at the Wyoming State Archives, Museums and Historical Department in Cheyenne, for access to important files and to the staff at Coe Library, University of Wyoming. Dr. Raymond J. DeMallie, Professor of Anthropology at Indiana University, was of great personal assistance to me, providing source material, encouragement and manuscript critiques. Special thanks to Dr. T. A. Larson, historian, of Laramie and to N. Scott Momaday, artist and author, of Tucson, Arizona, for manuscript reading. I am indebted to Homer Robinson, former superintendent at Devils Tower National Monument, for the time he took for personal interviews and for manuscript critiques on more than one occasion, and to his wife, Gisele, for her hospitality and fine art work. William Pierce, current Superintendent at Devils Tower National Monument, who allowed me access to Park Service photo files, and Dick Guilmette, author and Head Ranger at Devils Tower National Monument, who provided photo assistance and transport of Park Service negatives, also deserve my thanks. Of particular assistance in locating information about the

George Hopkins saga were Jerre Jones of Casper, former editor of the *Casper Journal*, who hand-carried valuable documents to me, and Earl Brockelsby and Reta Mae Maierhauser of Reptile Gardens in Rapid City, who made available personal scrapbook materials and photographs. My appreciation to Martin Russell, photography instructor at Casper College, who introduced me to the wonders of photography, and to three other friends and teachers of writing and literature who offered encouragement over a period of years: the late Peggy Simson Curry, author and Poet Laureate; and two professors of English at the University of Wyoming, Robert Roripaugh and Walter Edens. For their assistance with Indian background and Indian names for Devils Tower, many thanks to Joe Medicine Crow, Lodge Grass, Montana; Austin Two Moons, Northern Cheyenne Reservation, Montana; Arnold Headley, Ethete, Wyoming and to Harold Shunk, Rapid City, for background on White Bull.

Thanks also to Barb and Tom Rea of Casper and Patsy Parkin of Wheatland, for galley reading. Last, thanks to my friend and editor, Nancy Curtis of High Plains Press.

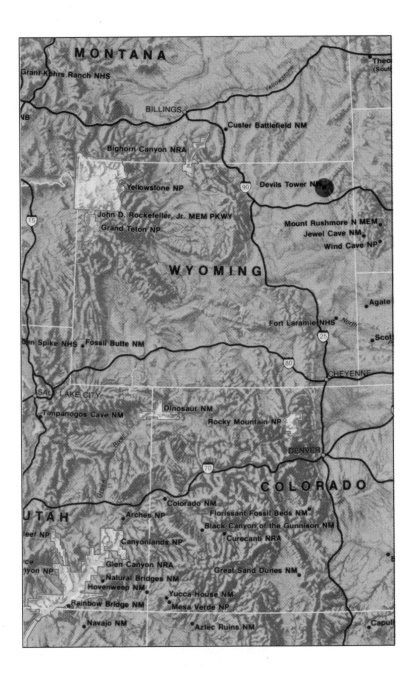

Well-known photographer J. E. Stimson of Cheyenne captured the mystery of Devils Tower in this 1903 photograph. *(Photograph by J. E. Stimson, Wyoming State Archives, Museums and Historical Department.)*

*There are things in nature that engender an
awful quiet in the heart of man; Devils Tower
is one of them.*

N. Scott Momaday
The Way to Rainy Mountain

Brief Geology

As we drive north on Wyoming's hilly Highway 24, glimpses of Devils Tower seem to play tag with the car. Now you see it— thimble-sized—now you don't. Around a sudden curve of highway on the right the gray tower rises, closer now. To the left and sloping upward are the Missouri Buttes, the highest domes like two small, bluish waves frozen on the horizon. We pull off onto a turnout facing a fresh wind, absorbing the clean sky. Light shifts, and the tower appears more brown in the distance.

Larger now with every mile, Devils Tower begins to resemble its photographs. It guards the prairie dog village in the meadow below the base as we become acquainted with a California couple and their two young sons. We suggest they hike the mile-long trail through the forest around the tower base. Later, they brake beside us in the visitor center parking lot, unpacking cameras and binoculars. Climbers are up today, red and green and white specks against the stark rock tower.

"Wow! I didn't know it was this big," says their freckle-faced ten-year-old.

Up close, Devils Tower is almost overwhelming. Emanating from the sheer, columned rock is a sense of peace and power, majesty as well as mystery. A creation of time and weather, it dominates the Belle Fourche Valley.

Geologists believe that Devils Tower looks much the same today as it did ten thousand years ago. But how did the rock

21

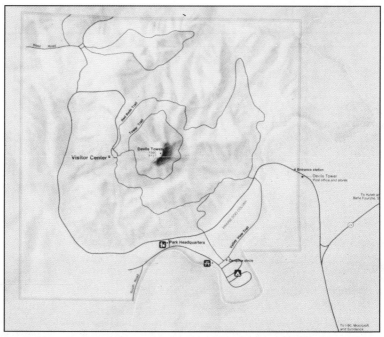

Our nation's first National Monument, Devils Tower was set aside in
1906 by the Antiquities Act, signed by President Theodore Roosevelt.
The monument grounds cover about two square miles near the middle
of Crook County. A clerical error omitted the apostrophe in "Devils"
and it has never been inserted. *(National Park Service)*

tower get that way?

Its geologic history is related to the formation of the Black
Hills, of which it is a part. Two-thirds of the Black Hills (about
120 miles long and 60 miles wide) lie in South Dakota; the rest
lie in Wyoming.

Both science and tradition explain the land form, these Hills
that rise like an island in the Great Plains. Geologists in 1875
compared the Black Hills to a blister, a bulge on the earth with
an enclosed granite core surrounded by a limestone rim.

Within the limestone rim—called Pahasapa Limestone for the
Sioux word meaning "Black Hills"—the granite core of the Hills
crests near South Dakota's Mount Rushmore National Monument

The Missouri Buttes, five dome-shaped formations which rise about four miles northwest of Devils Tower, have the same composition. Both the Missouri Buttes and Devils Tower are composed of a crystalline rock called phonolite porphyry. They share a common magma. *(National Park Service)*

at Harney Peak, 7,242 feet above sea level. The Wyoming portion of the Hills slopes down. The higher peaks of the Bear Lodge Mountains just inside the state border are some five hundred feet lower than Harney Peak. West of Wyoming's Bear Lodge Mountains are flat, open meadows and gently rolling hills.

Sioux and Cheyenne Indian legends explain it this way. The Black Hills were created, they say, during a Great Race between all the animals of the world. So great was their weight and speed that the land sank down and mountains rose inside the "race track," *kiinyanka ocanku*, as the Sioux designate the foothills surrounding the Black Hills. Western outliers of the Hills, Devils Tower and the Missouri Buttes lie outside this rim.

Hundreds of millions of years ago, limestone covered this region, laid down by ancient seas that rose and retreated, leaving layers of soil and sediment. At times the land thrust higher than the water. Erosion etched deeply into the old sea floors.

Some fifty to sixty million years ago both the Black Hills and the Rocky Mountains were formed. Colossal pressures uplifted waves of molten rock or magma, perhaps miles across. Soft surface rock layers buckled and split. Cracks opened. Fingers of magma reached upward through the cracks. Some became volcanoes. Studies conducted in the 1950s suggested that the flow beneath Devils Tower may have stopped about a thousand feet below the surface.

According to that theory, there the magma cooled, hardened and contracted. Underground, Devils Tower's unique four-, five-, and six-sided columns took shape. For centuries sediment covered the formation. Millions more years of erosion wore away the sandstone, limestone and shale. Over time, the Belle Fourche River carved away softer rock, revealing the tower. When first exposed, the tower was broad and low. Today the weathered upper portion appears rougher, more brittle. The tower now rises 1,282 feet above the river.

Devils Tower owes its striking appearance to different rates of rock erosion. Bright bands of softer red, yellow-green and gray sedimentary rock (sandstone, shale and gypsum) exposed in the lower part of the monument offer sharp contrast to the hard, gray-brown igneous rock of the upper tower.

Additional mid-50s research as well as a 1980 study indicate that Devils Tower and the Missouri Buttes, roughly four miles to the northwest, have the same composition. Both are a crystalline rock called phonolite porphyry. Possibly both formations are remnants of a laccolith, a tubular igneous formation thickest in the middle with a relatively flat floor. Like branches of the same stone tree, they share a common magma.

A detailed study conducted by Don L. Halvorson of Grand Forks, North Dakota, and presented in his doctoral dissertation in 1980 reintroduces a theory first proposed a century ago.

This view of Devils Tower shows its tear-shaped acre and a half top which is 5,117 feet above sea level. The tower rises 867 feet from the base. Base diameter is about 1,000 feet. Geologists believe that Devils Tower looks much the same today as it did 10,000 years ago. They are still debating the exact story of its origin. *(American Heritage Center, University of Wyoming)*

Halvorson's paper concludes that both Devils Tower and the Missouri Buttes are necks of extinct volcanoes which were later exposed by erosion. Varying rates of cooling and shrinkage could have formed the columns. Perhaps the full geological story is not yet known, but striking similarities do exist between volcanic necks discovered in the mountains of New Mexico and Wyoming's Devils Tower and Missouri Buttes.

Encircled by streams, the five dome-shaped Missouri Buttes, approximately a half-mile apart, rise up on private land near the divide between the headwaters of the Little Missouri River and the Belle Fourche River. Rock debris, similar to that around the tower base, dams a stream on the southwest, forming a small lake.

Long before white settlement, Crow Indian people called the most prominent domes "Two Buttes." Sioux people knew them as "Tipi Pole Buttes" because they went there to cut tipi poles. Geologists, in an 1890 report, noted that "Indians [no tribe given] called [the Missouri Buttes] 'buttes which look at each other.' "

Viewed from Hulett, the two most northerly peaks of the Missouri Buttes formation rise like clenched fists. Devils Tower juts up below them like a tiny thumb. Early travelers crossing to the north often spotted the Missouri Buttes but failed to see the tower, some four hundred feet lower.

To today's hikers, the chunks of rock debris and fragments of broken columns along the man-made trail that circles the tower base may seem to form a mountain. But geologists say the amount of rubble is small, suggesting that the tower has not been heavily eroded and was never much larger than it is today. Some of the larger fallen columns measure eight feet in diameter, and several are fourteen feet long.

But no new columns have fallen since records have been kept, in the last one hundred years. Nor has the prediction of a South Dakota historian come true. In 1899, Annie D. Tallent in *The Black Hills or the Last Hunting Ground of the Dacotahs* noted that the rock tower was "gradually disintegrating and falling

DEPARTMENT OF THE INTERIOR.
GENERAL LAND OFFICE.

DEVILS TOWER
NATIONAL MONUMENT,
WYOMING.

WARNING.

NOTICE IS HEREBY GIVEN that any person or persons who injure or destroy or, without specific authority from the Secretary of the Interior, excavate or appropriate any historic or prehistoric ruin, monument, object of antiquity, or of scientific interest, for the protection of which this reservation was created, will be subject to arrest and punishment under the provisions of the acts of Congress approved February 6, 1905, and June 8, 1906.

APPLICATIONS FOR PERMITS under the provisions of section 3 of the act of June 8, 1906, from reputable museums, universities, colleges, or other recognized scientific institutions, or their duly authorized agents, will be considered by the Secretary of the Interior.

FRED DENNETT,
Commissioner.

Approved, November 6, 1908.
JAMES RUDOLPH GARFIELD,
Secretary of the Interior.

Reports of acts of vandalism at Devils Tower filtered to Washington officials. The Department of Interior posted warning signs to discourage vandals. *(Wyoming State Archives, Museums and Historical Department)*

away, and will doubtless eventually crumble to a confused pile of broken rocks.''

For decades, there was speculation as to what lay on top of the tower.

Devils Tower National Monument, the first to be set aside in 1906 by the Antiquities Act which authorized President Theodore Roosevelt to designate "historical landmarks, historic and pre-historic structures, and other objects of scientific interest," now covers about two square miles near the middle of Crook County. This land once lay within the Great Sioux Reservation as unceded Indian Territory, with nearly one-fourth of present northeastern Wyoming and a wedge of southeastern Montana. Here, according to the Treaty of 1868, Sioux and Cheyenne Indians would be allowed to hunt without white interference, from north of the North Platte River and east of the summits of the Big Horn Mountains.

But many generations before that time people from the far north, the eastern prairies, the southwest were here. Shoshone, Comanche, Kiowa and Kiowa-Apache; Blackfoot, Piegan and Pawnee; Arikara, Crow, Arapaho, Cheyenne and Sioux people came here to hunt for buffalo, deer and other game. The valley was a favorite camping spot.

Their ancestors first watched the play of light and shadow upon the gray rock tower, as the morning sun defined it; the midday sun etched shadows along the crevices; late afternoon sun warmed the gray rock from yellow to a deep, glowing gold.

Many tribes had names for the tower, and it inspired in them a number of legends.

Works Cited

Geological information about Devils Tower is taken primarily from Charles S. Robinson's *Geology of Devils Tower National Monument, Wyoming* (Casper: National Park Service and Devils Tower Natural History Association, n.d.). See also Don L. Halvorson's "Geology and Petrology of the Devils Tower, Missouri Buttes and Barlow Canyon Area, Crook County, Wyoming," Ph.D. dissertation, University of North Dakota, 1980. See Charles S. Robinson, William J. Mapel and Maximilian H. Bergdahl's *Stratigraphy and Structure of the Northern and Western Flanks of the Black Hills Uplift, Wyoming, Montana and South Dakota,* Geological Survey Professional Paper 404 (Washington: U.S. Government Printing Office, 1964). Older sources of geological information include Thomas A. Jagger's "The Laccoliths of the Black Hills," U.S.G.S. 21st Annual Report (Washington: 1899-1900). Also Richard Irving Dodge's *The Black Hills* (New York: James Miller, 1876). Indian legends pertaining to formation of the Black Hills can be found in James LaPointe's *Legends of the Lakota* (San Francisco: Indian Historian Press, 1976). See also John Stands in Timber and Margot Liberty's *Cheyenne Memories* (Lincoln: University of Nebraska, Bison Books, 1972). Another older book, Annie D. Tallent's *The Black Hills or the Last Hunting Ground of the Dacotahs* (1899. Reprint New York: Arno Press, 1975) contains some references to Devils Tower. Indian names for the Missouri Buttes can be found in an unpublished manuscript by Dick Stone, "History of Devils Tower" (Cheyenne: Wyoming State Archives, Museums and Historical Department, n.d.) Microfilm. Much interesting information on Indian Treaty rights pertaining to the Black Hills has been assembled in editor Roxanne Dunbar Ortiz's *The Great Sioux Nation: Sitting in Judgment on America* (Berkeley: Moon Books, Inc., 1977).

Early Days and Legends

For most of the 1700s, the Crows and Kiowas together controlled the Black Hills of present-day South Dakota and northeastern Wyoming. So many grizzly bears roamed the slopes and ridges, Crow people called Devils Tower *Dabicha Asow,* "Bear's Lair."

The Crows' long migration into the area began some time in the 1500s when they left Canada, leading their dogs. They remained in northeastern North Dakota for half a century, dividing into separate, smaller tribal groups several times. Those who stayed behind were called Hidatsas. Others journeyed up the Missouri River. They called themselves Absarokas, the Raven people. The Absarokas also separated several times.

Somewhere on the Powder River, in Wyoming in the late 1700s, two groups of Absarokas met. One group, the River Crows, returned to the Missouri River. The second group, who stayed between Montana's Musselshell River and Wyoming's Powder River, were known as Mountain Crows.

From here, the Mountain Crows spread out, sometimes camping in the valley near Devils Tower, where game was plentiful along the Belle Fourche River.

Many years later, an old Crow Woman, Kills-Coming-to-the-Birds, spoke at a Fourth of July celebration in 1932 at Crow Agency, Montana. Among listeners was Gillette resident Dick Stone, who assembled a remarkable collection of legends and recollections about Devils Tower.

"I was at (Devils Tower) and saw them chasing a bear," she said in the Crow language. Chief Max Big Man interpreted, adding that Kills-Coming-to-the-Birds was a young woman "when the stars fell" in 1833, the great meteor shower seen throughout North America.

She told listeners her people believed Devils Tower was "put there by the Great Spirit for a special reason, because it was different from other rocks." And for this reason, she said, it was looked on as a holy place. The Crows went there to worship and to fast. She told of stone "dream houses" built near there.

The wife of White Man Runs Him, interviewed at the same time, described the rock dream houses as about as long as a man. In these, she said, a man could lie down with his head to the east and his feet to the west, "like the rising and setting sun."

Then, Rides the White Hip Horse told the following legend which Dick Stone transcribed, with Goes to Magpie interpreting.

"Once when some Crows were camped at 'Bear's House,' two little girls were playing around some big rocks there. There were lots of bears living around that big rock, and one big bear, seeing the girls alone, was going to eat them. The big bear was just about to catch the girls when they saw him. The girls were scared and the only place they could get was on top of one of the rocks around which they had been playing.

"The girls climbed the rock, but still the bear could catch them. The Great Spirit, seeing the bear was about to catch the girls, caused the rock to grow up out of the ground. The bear kept trying to jump to the top of the rock, but he just scratched the rock and fell down on the ground. The claw marks are on the rock now. The rock kept growing until it was so high that the bear could not get the girls.

"The two girls are still on top of the rock."

So awesome to the Kiowas was Devils Tower—known as *Tsoa-ai*, "tree rock"—that when they lived nearby two centuries ago a legend developed.

Generations after Kiowa people were living on Oklahoma's

Chief Max Big Man served as interpreter at a Fourth of July celebration held at Crow Agency, Montana, in 1932. Several Devils Tower legends and other recollections were told in the Crow language to visitors. *(The Montana Historical Society)*

southern plains, storytellers who had never seen the rock tower told of it, the streams and forests of the Black Hills—*Ts' ooukhou k'oup,* "Black Rock Mountains,"—and their good friends, the Crows. Researching for a scholarly article published in the late 1930s, anthropologist John P. Harrington noted that origin memories of American Indian people reveal none anywhere "as bright—and remote—"as the Kiowa memories of their days in the Black Hills and at Devils Tower.[1]

In *The Way to Rainy Mountain,* contemporary Kiowa author and Pulitzer-prize-winning novelist N. Scott Momaday recorded the story of his people's long migration. The Kiowas came from the north with dogs and sledges. With them was another people, the Kiowa Apaches, who retained a separate language. Unlike other peoples who lived east of the Mississippi and cultivated corn, the Kiowas have no tradition as farmers. Always they have been hunters.

It was on a hunting trip that a division of the Kiowas occurred. Two rival chiefs argued over possession of an antelope. Angry at losing, one chief and his people withdrew to the northwest. They were not seen again. The others moved southeast and crossed the Yellowstone River where they met the Crows who let them stay close by, about or before 1700.

Eventually, near the end of the 1700s, pressures from other tribes drove the Kiowas and Kiowa-Apaches from the Black Hills. With them they carried their memories, some Crow children given them by Crow people so that each would know the other's language and—among their stories—the legend of *Tsoa-ai,* recorded in Momaday's *The Way to Rainy Mountain.*

"Eight children were there at play, seven sisters and their brother. Suddenly the boy was struck dumb; he trembled and began to run upon his hands and feet. His fingers became claws,

---

[1]Harrington's article also notes the following name difference for Devils Tower: *T'sou' a'e,* literally translated as "aloft on the rock." John P. Harrington, "Kiowa Memories of the Northland," *So Live the Works of Men,* ed. D. D. Brand and F. E. Harvey (Albuquerque: University of New Mexico Press, 1939), pp. 169–170.

and his body was covered with fur. Directly there was a bear where the boy had been. The sisters were terrified; they ran, and the bear after them. They came to the stump of a great tree, and the tree spoke to them. It bade them climb upon it, and as they did so it began to rise into the air. The bear came to kill them, but they were just beyond its reach. It reared against the tree and scored the bark all around with its claws. The seven sisters were borne into the sky, and they became the stars of the Big Dipper."[2]

Momaday's Kiowa name, given him at six months, is *Tsoatalee,* or "Rock Tree Boy."

Speaking at a library convention in Riverton, Wyoming, in April of 1982, Momaday told the legend and added that the story itself "is a great act of the imagination, and it justifies the human spirit, in the way that stories do. Not only did the Kiowas who beheld this great, strange sight in nature account for it, explain it to themselves, appropriate it into their own experience, but they related themselves forever to the stars."

Old stories tell of Arapaho migrations across what we know as the Bering Strait or Aleutian Islands. They roamed from the Lake Michigan area, eventually crossing the Missouri into the Black Hills and south to Colorado. *Woox-niii-non,* "Bear's Tipi," the Arapahoes called Devils Tower.

Skillful traders with huge horse herds, they ranged thousands of miles hunting buffalo and trapping beaver to trade for guns, ammunition, knives and kettles. From Mexican traders they obtained blankets, flour, beads and silver bridles. Their migration into the Black Hills preceded that of the Cheyennes, with whom they later allied. At peace with most other tribes, they may have joined the Cheyennes in order to preserve and protect their horse herds and immense, southern supply lines.

Beginning about 1826, part of the Araphoes and Cheyennes left the Black Hills country, settling south between the Arkansas

---

[2]N. Scott Momaday, *The Way to Rainy Mountain* (Albuquerque: University of New Mexico, 1969), p. 8.

and Platte Rivers. Since 1876, many Northern Arapahoes have lived in central Wyoming on the Wind River Reservation.

At his home near St. Michael's Mission in Ethete, Wyoming, 81-year old Sherman Sage related several incidents to Dick Stone during the summer of 1932. With the help of interpreter Otto Hungary, Sage told listeners that his grandfather, Drying-Up-Hide, was buried near Devils Tower. And he told of his grandfather's great power over animals.

Near the tower, Sage said, his grandfather once built a trap with tree branches. He went out to sing to the antelope, buffalo and deer. Four times he repeated his song, each time in a higher key. The first time the animals heard it, they stopped eating. At the second singing, they raised their heads and looked around. After the third repetition, they walked towards the trap. As Drying-Up-Hide finished the fourth singing, the animals walked into the trap.

Sage sang for listeners his grandfather's song, then told a story he had received from his father, Straight Old Man, when he was nine years old.

"An Arapaho lodge was camped at Bear's Tipi. The father of this lodge was a headman and had seven children, five boys and two girls. The two girls made an arrangement between themselves that the one who found the end bone (rib) of a buffalo should receive the most favors from the brothers. The boys often made trips to other tribes. After a long search, one of the girls found an end bone of a buffalo, and on picking it up, she turned into a bear and made some scratches on her sister's back. The bear-girl told her sister, 'If you tell, the dogs will howl and this will be a signal, so I will know if you have told.' The sister did tell and when (the children) heard the dogs howl and give the signal, they were scared and started to run.

"The bear-girl heard the signal and ran after them. The girl who had told was carrying a ball in her hand which she dropped and accidentally kicked. The ball bounced up on the big, high rock. The bear-girl climbed to the top of the big, high rock and told her family that there would be seven stars in the shape of a

The peaceful magnificence of the tower, captured in 1903 by photographer J. E. Stimson, makes it easy to understand why Indian peoples sought spiritual solace in the Black Hills. (*J. E. Stimson photograph; Wyoming State Archives, Museums and Historical Department*)

diamond appearing in the east and the first star out would be brighter than the other stars. This first star would be called Broken Chest Star. From this time on, the Arapahoes called this big, high rock 'Bear's Tipi.' ''

The Cheyennes first lived in the woodlands of southeastern Minnesota. Pushed west in the 1700s, they allied themselves with agricultural tribes of the Missouri River. Along with Mandans, Hidatsas and Arikaras, they built earth lodges and cultivated crops, relying on dogs for transportation.

Displaced still farther west by tribal wars, the Cheyennes moved from east of the Black Hills, skirting the southern end and entering Wyoming's Powder River Basin, the area known today as portions of the state's Sheridan, Johnson, Campbell, Weston, Converse, Niobrara and Crook Counties. Throughout several generations, bands of nomadic Cheyennes and others remained on the Missouri in agricultural villages.

By 1830, the Cheyennes had enough horses to become completely nomadic. About this time they separated into two divisions, the southern division ranging into eastern Colorado and western Kansas and Oklahoma. The Northern Cheyenne ranged from northeastern Colorado across Wyoming's Powder River Basin to Montana, mingling freely with their allies, the Dakotas and Arapahoes.

But even before the Cheyennes had horses, they camped by *Na Kovea*, ''Bear's Lodge.'' Here Sweet Medicine, their great culture hero, lay dying. He had lived, they said, four generations and gave to the people the Four Sacred Arrows. He founded warrior societies, tribal governing bodies, and taught them many special laws and ceremonies.

But when he knew his death was near, he instructed his people to build him a cedar pole hut covered with grass and bark. There he lay on a bed of soft grass. Then he told them to make a new camp several miles away, but to return when this was done so that he might speak with them one last time.

Sweet Medicine gave his final, dark prophecy. He foretold

the coming of the horse; the disappearance of the old ways and the buffalo, to be replaced by slick animals with split hoofs the people must learn to eat—cattle. And he told them of white men, strangers called Earth Men who could fly above the earth, take thunder for light; men who would dig at the earth and drain it, until it was dead.

They left him there in the hut by Devils Tower. Sweet Medicine was not seen again, but his prophecy is remembered by the Cheyennes today.

Many Northern Cheyennes live on their present reservation in southeastern Montana.

Two remarkable legends of *Na Kovea,* "Bear's Lodge," were related to Dick Stone by men of the Northern Cheyenne tribe: one in private the summer of 1932 and another the following year in a large council tipi, with the aid of prompters.

Summer, 1932: Young Bird, a medicine man and healer, made five marks in the dirt before beginning the story. These marks may refer to old rituals which accompanied certain old, very holy stories.

Before beginning, a storyteller would smooth the ground before him, making two marks with his right thumb, two with the left and another with both thumbs together, next performing other motions. He would touch the five marks on the ground with both hands and rub them together, passing his hands over his head and body. This signified that as the Creator had made people's limbs and bodies, so had He also formed the earth and He was a witness to the particular story.

"This is a true story," Young Bird said. Samuel Weasel Bear acted as interpreter.

"A band of Cheyenne Indians went on one of the visits to 'Bear's Tipi' to worship the Great Spirit, as did many other tribes before the white man came. The Cheyenne braves took their families with them as they felt that would be safe, as Bear's Tipi was a holy place.

"After having camped there for several days, one of the

Cheyenne braves noticed that his wife was often gone from camp, staying away for a short time. As time went on, he noticed that she was gone longer than before. This brave could not understand why his wife should be gone from their lodge so much, as he had always been devoted to her and being a good hunter, as well as a brave warrior, she always had much buffalo, antelope and deer meat. He furnished her fine skins to make nice clothes.

"Becoming suspicious that some other brave in his band might be courting his wife, he watched to see what man was missing when his wife left camp. He found that no man was missing when his wife was gone. This man also saw that his wife had a skin over her shoulders now that she did not wear before coming to this camp.

"One day when she had been gone longer than usual, he lay in wait for her. On her return he asked her where she had been and what drew her from camp so much of the time. She would not answer any of his questions. Then the man became mad and tore the skin from her shoulders and saw that she was covered with scratches.

"He demanded that she tell him which man had abused her. Becoming frightened at the way her husband was acting, she told him that she had been chased by a very big bear that lived in the big rock. The bear had no mate and had become infatuated with her while she was out gathering fruit. Fearing for the safety of the camp, she had submitted to the bear's embraces, which accounted for the scratches on her shoulders.

"Then the warrior told his wife to lead him to the bear so he could kill it. When they found the bear, the man had great fear because the bear was big, very big. The bear slapped the woman with his paw and changed her into a bear. The man ran to the camp to get the rest of the braves to help him kill the big bear.

"They found the bear had crawled into a cave, leaving his hind feet in the door. The bear's feet were so big that nobody could get past them. They could not get close enough to the bear to kill him, so they shot at his feet to make him come out. When the bear came out, he was so big that all the warriors were scared and climbed up on a big rock.

"These men were so scared that they prayed to the Great Spirit to save them. In answer to their prayers the rock began to grow up out of the ground and when it stopped it was very high. The bear jumped at the men and on the fourth jump, his claws were on the top. The Great Spirit had helped the men and now they had great courage and they shot the bear and killed him . . .

"After that the bear-woman made this big rock her home, so the Cheyennes called it 'Bear Tipi'."

Summer: 1933. Invited by Young Bird to return to Lame Deer, Montana, for more stories, Dick Stone and other researchers were saddened to learn that he had died of pneumonia the previous winter. Accompanied by well-known interpreter Willis Rowland (High Forehead), they were sent to talk with a Cheyenne named Limpy, a veteran of the Custer battle.[3]

Field notes describing the meeting with Limpy indicate that

---

[3]As a young boy Limpy participated in the Battle of the Rosebud (June 17, 1876)—his first experience in battle—and the Custer battle a week later. Limpy was among those Cheyennes who aided Thomas B. Marquis in his research at Custer Battlefield during the 1920s. See Marquis' book *The Cheyennes of Montana* (Algonac: Reference Publications, Inc., 1978). Willis Rowland (High Forehead) was the son of William Rowland (Long Knife), who married into the Cheyenne tribe in 1850 and homesteaded in the Tongue River area even before the reservation was established in 1884. Both men interpreted at Lame Deer, Montana, for many years. Credit for assistance as interpreters to "William Rowland and his sons" appears in the foreword of George Bird Grinnell's classic *The Cheyenne Indians: Their History and Ways of Life*, 2 vols. (1923; reprint, Lincoln: University of Nebraska, 1972). Willis Rowland served also as interpreter for other well-known researchers, and received credit in forewords of the following books: E. Adamson Hoebel's *The Cheyennes, Indians of the Great Plains* (1906; reprint, New York: Holt, Rinehart and Winston, 1978) and also Karl N. Llewellyn and E. Adamson Hoebel's *The Cheyenne Way* (Norman: University of Oklahoma, 1941).

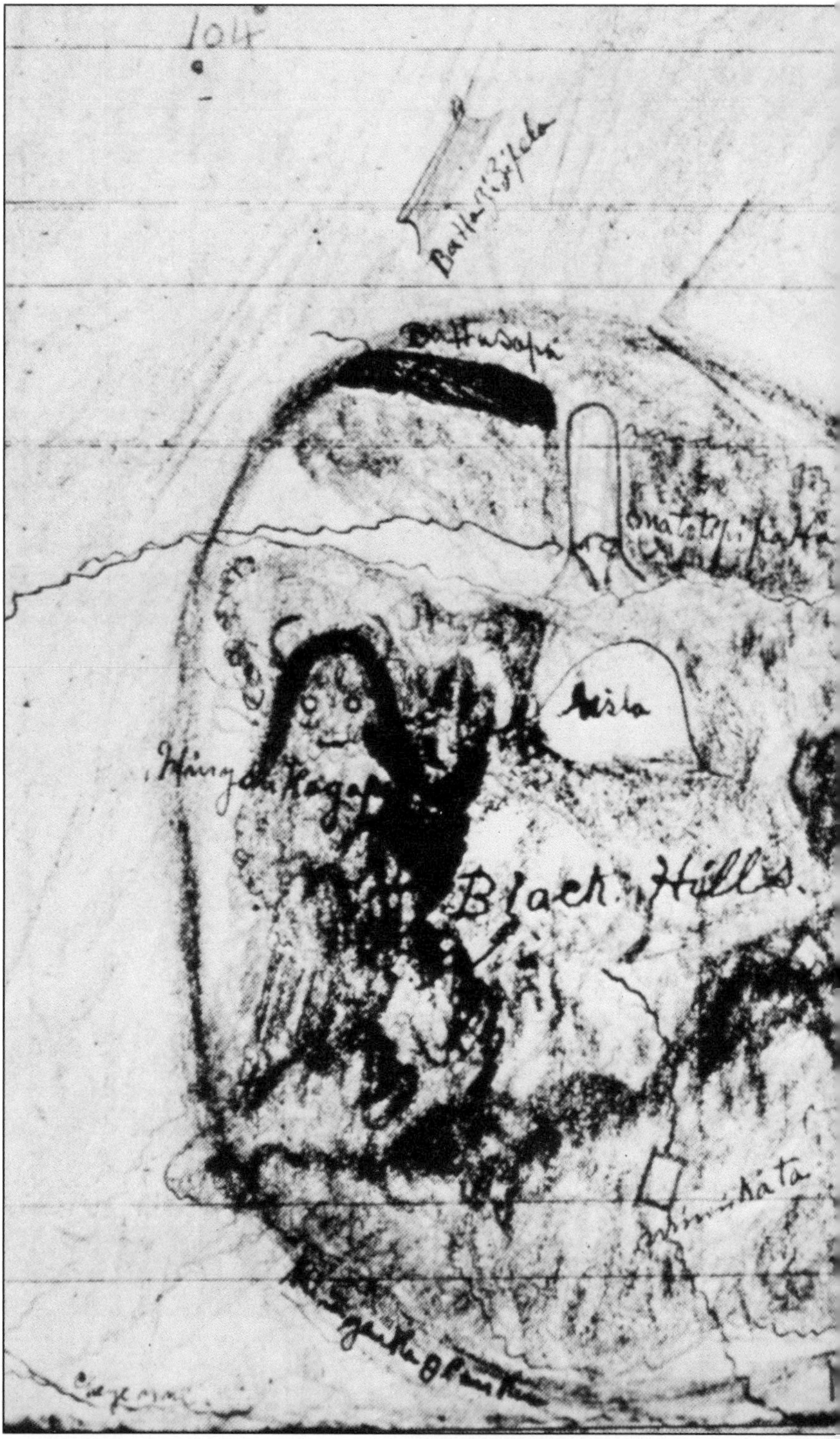
104
Black Hills

Overleaf:

This topographical representation of the Black Hills was drawn by Amos Bad Heart Bull (also known as Eagle Lance), an Oglala Sioux from the Pine Ridge Reservation who was born in Wyoming in 1869. It is one of a series of four hundred drawings with written notations collected in his ledger book, probably drawn between 1890–1910. A talented artist with a great interest in recording his people's history, he kept records primarily for himself, having collected information from his father and uncles: Bad Heart Bull the elder, Only Man, Little Shield, He Dog and Short Bull. Though he apparently received little formal schooling, he learned on his own to write in Lakota, using the Riggs system of writing which was instituted by missionaries after reservations were established. Amos Bad Heart Bull served as scout at Fort Robinson in 1890–91 and perhaps learned to write also in English during that time.

Ringing the Black Hills is *Kiinyanka Ocanku*, the "race track." Points recorded to the north of the Black Hills are *Baha Zizipela* (Slim Buttes), and to the northeast, *Mikiyan Paha* (Thunder Butte). Drawn inaccurately within the Hills is the shaft of *Mato Tipi Paha* (Bear Lodge Butte), which rises from the eastern Wyoming plains. Also within the "race track" to the north and colored black is *Baha Sapa* (Black Mountain or Black Butte). Below Bear Lodge, in the center, is *Re Sla* (Bear Mountain or "Old Baldy" on some maps.) To the west, drawn as a horned head, is *Hinyankaga Paha* (Ghost Butte). Due east of Ghost Butte and outside the "race track" is *Mato Paha* (Bear Butte) near present Sturgis, South Dakota. Farther south the small white rectangular area is designated *Mini Kata* (Hot Springs), today Hot Springs, South Dakota. Southeast of here, colored dark, is *Pte Tali Yapa* (Buffalo Gap). A small circle outside the "race track" denotes both *Miniluzahan* a shortened version of "fast water," and "Rapid City." From *A Pictographic History of the Oglala Sioux*, by Amos Bad Heart Bull, text by Helen Blish, by permission of the University of Nebraska Press. Copyright © 1967 by the University of Nebraska Press

the "mention of this place (Devils Tower) seemed to carry Limpy back to the days when his people wandered free and happy over the hills and prairies. His face turned to the east and we saw that his thoughts were far away. Limpy was silent for so long that (Willis Rowland) recalled the old man from his dreams of the days that used to be."

"There are some things we don't like to talk about," Limpy said. "That was a very holy place to us." But when reminded by Rowland that the younger Cheyennes didn't know the stories, and if they were lost, would never know them again, Limpy said, "It is true."

Not wanting to be distracted from Sun Dance ceremonies which were beginning, he asked them to come back with "meat, some bread, some coffee and something sweet," and he would tell them all he knew about "Bear's House"—if they were "men enough to stay up all night." He added that some of the other old men would help him tell it straight. "If I don't tell it straight," Limpy said, "I will be punished."

Three weeks later, July 21, the group returned. Limpy had sent word he was too old to make the long trip from his home back to the campground, but Rowland had another plan so that the group might get the stories they had come for.

After the dancing that same night, an old man named Medicine Top went through the village announcing in Cheyenne that tomorrow he would tell the story about "Bear's Tipi," and that he would tell it "straight and true."

The next morning many Cheyennes came to the council tipi to hear Medicine Top's story. Medicine Top said that the legend had been told to him by his father. Before telling it, he prayed to the Great Spirit, who gave them food and clothing, to "look down upon them and help them tell the story straight and true."

As he began, in the Cheyenne tongue, he also told the story in sign language. Rowland carefully interpreted. Pine and Spotted Black Bird acted as prompters.

"Once there was a man and his wife. The wife went out to

fix the smoke wings to prevent smoke in the lodge. While she was doing this a big bear came and carried her off. This man had six brothers of which he was the oldest. After losing his wife, this man mourned greatly. He would go out and cry out to the bear and defy him.

"The bear took this woman to a cave that was his home. The youngest of the brothers told his oldest brother to make him a bow and four arrows. Two of the arrows were to be feathered with eagle feathers and painted red with the paint they got from the hills. The other two arrows were to be feathered with buzzard feathers and painted black. He had two red arrows and two black ones. The arrows were not pointed. The oldest brother was told to make them blunt and not sharpen them. The seven brothers then went after the oldest one's wife, who had been carried off by a big bear. The youngest man told his brothers to take plenty of arrows, to fill their quivers full. The young brother had only four arrows, the two red ones and the two black ones. The others had as many as they wanted.

"When they got close to the bear's den, the youngest man told his brothers to sit down and stay there. This youngest brother had great power. He got up and walked around. He turned himself into a gopher and dug a hole to the bear's den big enough to bring the woman out. The bear that had taken the woman was lying with his head in the woman's lap. This man, who had changed himself into a gopher, had the power to put the rest of the bears in the den to sleep. He also had the power to put the big bear, that had stolen the woman, to sleep. The hole he had dug was just big enough to take the woman out. He then turned back into an Indian. He spoke to the woman and told her that he was there to take her back. He also told her that his oldest brother thought a lot of her and had been mourning for her. He told her to take her blanket and make a pillow out of it and put it under the bear's head. He then told her to crawl backwards into the hole he had dug. He took the woman out and they came to the place where he first went in. The six brothers were still sitting there. After they came out, the hole closed up.

"When this woman got out, she told those seven people that they had better be leaving, and leaving fast, because the big bear was one that could not be killed. Arrows would not go into him. The youngest brother, with the four arrows, kept looking back. The big bear got out of his den and walked around it. He found the trail where the Indians had left. He took the rest of the bears with him. This big bear was the leader. Soon the Indians saw the bears coming, and coming fast.

"Soon the Indians came to the place where 'Bear's Tipi' is today. The youngest brother always carried a small rock in his hand. He told the six other brothers and the woman to close their eyes. He sang a song and finished it. The others opened their eyes. The rock had grown in size. He sang four times and when he had finished, the rock was just as high as it is today. He was able to do this because he was a holy man.

"When the bears got up to the big rock, they all sat down in a line except the main one and he stood out in front. The bear called out, 'Let my woman come down.' The youngest Indian answered the bear, saying, 'You might be a holy being, but you cannot get her.' He mocked the bear about his power and being able to do almost anything. The brothers killed all of the bears except the leader. This bear growled and tried to get to the top of the rock by jumping. He could get up quite a ways but could not reach the top.

"While the bear was trying to get to the top of this big rock, the youngest brother shot a black arrow at him. It didn't hurt him. The bear got farther up every jump he made by taking a run. The bear's claws made the marks that are on the rock today. The third jump the bear made, the Indian shot a red arrow at him that didn't go in. The fourth jump the bear almost got there. This man shot him with the last arrow. It went into the top of the bear's head and came out below his jaw. This arrow killed the bear. The youngest brother then made a noise like a bald eagle and four of these eagles came there. The Indians took hold of the eagles' legs and were carried down to the ground.

"When they reached the ground the youngest man told his

Some Indian legends attribute the tower's columnar striations to claw marks gouged into the rock by a huge bear attempting to reach Indians atop the tower. (*Wyoming State Archives, Museums, and Historical Department*)

brothers to pack in a lot of wood and put it on top of the bear that had stolen the woman. They piled a lot of wood on him and then set it on fire. When the bear got red hot it popped. Small pieces, like beads of different colors, flew off of him. The youngest brother told the rest of them to put the pieces back into the fire with a stick. If they had put the pieces back into the fire with their hands, the bear would have come to life again. They burned the bear down to ashes.

"After this there were a lot of young bears running around there. The Indians killed all but two. The youngest brother talked to them. He told them not to bother the people any more. He cut their ears and tails off. That is why bears have short ears and no tails, to this day."

The Sioux can be traced back to the Mississippi-Ohio Valley. Some migrated east to the Atlantic, some to the Gulf Coast and others to the upper midwest and the plains. Cheyenne tradition says that the first Sioux people came into their camps on foot, seeking food and shelter, more of them coming every season.

Written records show that by 1750 various Sioux tribes had crossed the Missouri River. Within the next twenty years, the powerful Teton Sioux swept upward into northern Wyoming and southeastern Montana. Through the 1850s they dominated all sides of the Black Hills country.. Year after year, sometimes aided by Cheyennes and Arapahoes, Hunkpapa Sioux along with Minneconjous and Sans Arcs from the Belle Fourche River area crossed Powder River to attack the Crows.

One story, an outgrowth of these conflicts, tells of a Crow-Sioux encounter. It was related to Dick Stone by Lone Man, then 84 years old, at his home west of Oglala, on the Sioux Reservation in July, 1933. Daniel Stands was interpreter.

"A band of Sioux had their camp at *Mato Tipila,* Bear's Lodge. They had gone there to worship. A band of Crow Indians was near that place, and seeing the Sioux there, started to fight them, the Sioux and the Crow being hereditary enemies. The Crows attacked the Sioux camp which was in the timber at the foot of this rock (Devils Tower).

"After the fight had been going on all day, the Sioux had run out of arrows and then they were afraid that they would all be killed. At this time a big bear came out of the woods and told the Sioux to sit still and he would fight the Crows.

"The bear went out and fought the Crows, but being a holy bear, the Crows were not able to kill him. As soon as the Crows would shoot their arrows at the bear, he would pick them up and give them to the Sioux. When the sun went down, the Crows had not killed any of the Sioux and the big bear made them go away.''

Sitting Bull's two nephews, the Hunkpapa One Bull and well-known Minneconjou Chief White Bull, interviewed by Dick Stone as old men in 1934, recalled childhood memories and older stories of more peaceful days near Devils Tower.[4]

By the Belle Fourche River below the tower's base, the people often spent long winter months, One Bull said. Here they rested, hunting the plentiful game abounding there—buffalo, deer, elk, bear and mountain lions. The women tanned hides and made them into robes and buckskins. Beaver trapped along the streams were traded for "white man's goods" when traders came into the camps with oxen.

White Bull recalled a time in 1854 when Mexican traders came to sell blankets to Arapahoes camped with the Sioux. His father, Chief Makes Room, made friends with the traders, giving them skins and buffalo hides for beads, knives, Mexican bridles, powder and ammunition. White Bull told also of "honor men" among the people who went up close to Devils Tower for four-day periods, fasting and praying. There they slept on beds of sagebrush, taking no food or water during this time.

Once, five great Sioux leaders—Sitting Bull, Crazy Horse, Red Cloud, Gall and Spotted Tail—went there together to worship.

"We did not worship this butte, but worshipped our God," White Bull told listeners.

The following legend tells of such a vision quest.

"In the Sioux tribe long ago, there was a brave warrior who often went alone into the wilderness where he would fast and worship the Great Spirit in solitude. Being alone helped him strengthen his courage so that in the future he could carry out his plans.

"One day this warrior took his buffalo skull and went alone into the wilderness to worship. Standing at the base of *Mato Tipila* after he had worshipped for two days, he suddenly found himself on top of this high rock. He was very much frightened

---

[4]One Bull, *Tatanka Wanjila*, the son of Chief Makes Room and Pretty Feather (Sitting Bull's sister), was interviewed at a Hunkpapa Sioux camp near Miles City, Montana, on May 25, 1934, with Luke Eagle Man interpreting. He was adopted by Sitting Bull when he was four years old and raised as his son. Described as being small in stature, he was called brave and outgoing. He distinguished himself particularly at the Custer battle and went with Sitting Bull to Canada from 1877-1881. See Stanley Vestal's *Sitting Bull: Champion of the Sioux* (1932; reprint, Norman: University of Oklahoma, 1957). He was enrolled on tribal records as Henry Oscar One Bull. See also Sister Inez Hilger, "The Narrative of Oscar One Bull," *Mid-America, An Historical Review* 2d ser., 17, no. 3 (July 1946). White Bull, *Pte-san-hunka*, gave his statements at Little Eagle, South Dakota, in July, 1934. His son, George White Bull, acted as interpreter. White Bull was born in 1850, the son of Minneconjou Chief Makes Room and Good Feather Woman, Sitting Bull's younger sister. Vestal's *Sitting Bull: Champion of the Sioux* describes White Bull's participation in battle with Crows, Rees, Flatheads, Assiniboins and Shoshones, as well as a number of Indian-white battles, among them the Fetterman Massacre, the Wagon Box Fight, the Battle of the Little Big Horn. Vestal profiled White Bull in *Warpath: The True Story of the Sioux Wars as Told in a Biography of White Bull* (Boston: Houghton Mifflin, 1934.) White Bull himself wrote a book in 1931, based on a system developed by missionary Stephen R. Riggs in the 1890s. White Bull continued as a leader among his people during reservation days, joining the Indian police, serving as tribal judge and chairman of the tribal council. Active in church affairs, he spoke on several occasions regarding the Treaty of 1868 and participated in a reenactment of the Custer battle. His book, written in Lakota, was eventually published in the late 1960s: James Howard, translator and editor, *The Warrior Who Killed Custer* (Lincoln: University of Nebraska, 1968). White Bull died in 1946.

One Bull (*Tatanka Wanjila*) a Hunkpapa Sioux, participated in the Custer Battle and went to Canada with Sitting Bull, his adoptive father, from 1877–1881. During the 1930s, he told interviewers details of the early days when his people camped along the river below Devils Tower. *(South Dakota State Historical Society)*

as he did not know how he would get down. After appealing to the Great Spirit, he went to sleep. When he awoke, he was very glad to find that he was again at the base of this high rock.

"He saw that he was standing at the door of a big bear's lodge, as there were footprints of a very big bear there. He could tell that the cracks in the big rock were made by the big bear's claws. So he knew that all the time he had been on top of this big rock, he had been standing on a big bear's lodge.

"From this time on, his nation called this rock *Mato Tipila* and they went there to worship. The buffalo skull is still on top of this big, high rock."

Another legend of how Devils Tower came to be, recorded in James LaPointe's *Legends of the Lakota,* tells of the rescue of two little Sioux girls by Fallen Star.

The son of a Sioux girl and a strange young man who came from a world in the sky, Fallen Star was raised by adopted parents. From his youth he seemed destined for special ways. Not long after he attained manhood, Fallen Star returned to the sky from which, as a brilliant star, he would watch over all peoples of the earth.

One day as a band of Sioux moved toward the Black Hills to harvest fruit it happened. Two little girls wandered away over the rough, pine-studded ridges and were lost. Search parties went out. In the distance the girls were seen, surrounded by bears, with no one near enough to save them.

"Suddenly a voice from the blue sky spoke to the little girls, saying *Paha akili* (climb the hill). It had a strange effect on the attacking bears . . . they stood paralyzed, giving the little girls a chance to clamber up a small knoll.

"The girls huddled together on the hill and hid their faces from the angry bears, as once again the animals . . . began climbing after them. The earth shook and groaned, as the little knoll, commanded by the strange voice, began to rise out of the ground, carrying the children high into the air. Higher and higher the mound rose, as the frustrated bears growled and clawed at its sides. Sharp pieces of rock broke away from the rising spire and crashed down upon the angry bears.

White Bull (*Pte-san-hunka*), a Minneconjou chief, was a leader in prereservation days who also served as tribal judge and chairman of the tribal council. He was the nephew of Sitting Bull. He provided Wyoming researcher Dick Stone with information about Devils Tower. *(South Dakota State Historical Society)*

"The children were safe now from the snarling bears, but . . . how were they to get down? Appearing like tiny specks on top of a high, sharp mound, they kept their eyes tightly closed, not daring to look down. But the strange voice spoke again, saying, 'Do not cry. You will not fall. I have many pretty birds with me. Make friends with them, for soon you will ride upon a pretty bird . . .' "

"A covey of birds appeared. The kindly voice belonged to none other than Fallen Star. Molten rocks poured down the sides of the mound, burying the hungry bears. Each little girl now chose a pretty bird upon whose back she flew into the anxious arms of her frantic mother."

That was how the tower came to be, say Lakota legends. To prove it, there are deep crevices along the walls, claw marks made by huge bears long ago.[5]

Over the years as the tower became known to more and more white trappers and traders, translations of its Indian names— "bear's house," "bear's tipi," "dwelling place of the bear"— shifted slightly. On early maps its name appears as Bear Lodge.

[5]James LaPointe, *Legends of the Lakota* (San Francisco: Indian Historian Press, 1976) p. 67.

Works Cited

I am indebted to Joe Medicine Crow, Crow tribal historian of Lodge Grass, Montana, for the Crow word for Devils Tower— *Dabicha Asow*—whose other translations include "Bear's Home." For an interesting history of the Crow tribe see Cindy Buckingham, Jan Green, Geneva Stuart, Marlon Red Star, and Others, *A History of the Crow Indians Based on Written Sources: From the Roaming Days to the Reservation* (Lodge Grass: Lodge Grass Public Schools, 1971). All legends except where footnoted are from the same group of documents, letters and interviews collected by Dick Stone, *History of Devils Tower: 1804–1934* (Cheyenne: Wyoming State Archives, Museums and Historical Department, n.d.) Microfilm. Many of the legends collected by Stone are available in the chapbook *First Encounters: Indian Legends of Devils Tower* ([Devils Tower], Shirl [Shirley Rathbun], 1982). Information about the Kiowas was assembled from John P. Harrington's "Kiowa Memories of the Northland," *So Live the Works of Men,* edited by D. D. Brand and F. E. Harvey, (Albuquerque: University of New Mexico, 1939) as well as James Mooney's *Calendar History of the Kiowa Indians* (1898. Reprint Washington: Smithsonian Institution, 1979) and N. Scott Momaday's *The Way to Rainy Mountain* (Albuquerque: University of New Mexico, 1969). I am indebted to Arnold Headley, Northern Arapaho from Ethete, Wyoming, who provided the Arapaho name for Devils Tower, *Woox-niii-non.* Also of interest in regard to Indian occupation of the Black Hills area is *Archeology of the Eastern Powder River Basin,* George M. Zeimens and Danny M. Walker, editors, (Prepared for the Bureau of Land Management, 1977). I am indebted to Cheyenne tribal leader Austin Two Moons who provided the Cheyenne name, *Na Kovea,* for "Bear Lodge" (Devils Tower) at "Indian Awareness Week" at the Sheridan County Fullmer Public Library, July 30, 1982. Much information is available about the Cheyennes, including George Bird Grinnell's *The Cheyenne Indians: Their History and Ways of Life.* 2 vols. (1923. Reprint Lincoln: University of Nebraska, 1972);

Known to generations of Sioux as *Mato Paha* and to the Cheyenne as *Noaha-Vose* (Sacred Mountain), Bear Butte near Sturgis, South Dakota, is still the site of pilgrimages where people fast and pray. Bear Butte State Park is also a registered National Landmark. (*South Dakota State Historical Society*

E. Adamson Hoebel's *The Cheyennes: Indians of the Plains* (1906. Reprint New York: Holt, Rinehart and Winston, 1978); Thomas B. Marquis, *The Cheyennes of Montana* (Algonac: Reference Publications, Inc., 1978); Peter J. Powell's *Sweet Medicine: The Continuing Role of the Sacred Arrows, The Sun Dance and the Sacred Buffalo Hat in Northern Cheyenne History.* 2 vols. (Norman: University of Oklahoma, 1969); and John Stands in Timber and Margot Liberty's *Cheyenne Memories* (Lincoln: University of Nebraska, Bison Books, 1972). An undated letter to Dick Stone from Chief Luther Standing Bear, hereditary chief of the Oglala Sioux, states that *"Mato Tipila . . .* means dwelling place of the bears. *Tipila,* does not, strictly speaking, mean a lodge but rather a living place, or place where bears should live." See also James LaPointe's *Legends of the Lakota* (San Francisco: Indian Historian Press, 1976) and *Legends of the Mighty Sioux,* compiled by South Dakota Writers' Project Works Project Administration (1941. Reprint Sioux Falls: Fantab, Inc., 1960). Many books are available on the Sioux Indians, among them

Henry W. Hamilton and Jean Tyree Hamilton's *The Sioux of the Rosebud* (Norman: University of Oklahoma, 1971); Royal B. Hassrick's *The Sioux: Life and Customs of a Warrior Society* (Norman: University of Oklahoma, 1977); George E. Hyde's *A Life of George Bent: Written From His Letters* (Norman: University of Oklahoma, 1967); editor Roxanne Dunbar Ortiz's *The Great Sioux Nation: Sitting in Judgment on America* (Berkeley: Moon Books, Inc., 1977); and Stanley Vestal's *Sitting Bull: Champion of the Sioux* (1932. Reprint Norman: University of Oklahoma, 1957).

Exploration

Rumors of gold in the Black Hills had circulated for years: tales of rich lodes, nuggets for the taking, of Indians who shot gold-tipped arrows. Miners entering illegally in the 1850s reported finding rusted shovels and rotted sluice boxes, wooden beams with dates as old as 1803 carved into them.

Knowing they trespassed and violated existing treaties, several government-sponsored expeditions penetrated Indian country. Several came close to Bear Lodge and the Missouri Buttes. The first was in 1857.

Charged with looking for sites for possible military posts and assembling scientific information, Lieutenant G. K. Warren was ordered by the Secretary of War that spring to locate roadways that could connect Fort Laramie and South Pass to points farther east, and to explore the Black Hills. With him was veteran geologist Ferdinand V. Hayden, other scientists and an escort of thirty men of the Second Infantry.

Delayed at Fort Laramie because of a scarcity of supplies, Warren divided the party into two groups to cover more ground. On September 4, Warren, two topographers, a meteorologist, an Indian guide and seventeen packers headed north. They entered the Black Hills by a branch of Beaver Creek, continuing as far as Inyan Kara Mountain, some thirty miles southeast of Bear Lodge.

A force of angry Minneconjous—forty lodges—stopped them

at Inyan Kara. Later in the day more Hunkpapa and Sihasapa (Blackfoot Sioux) joined them. A large Sioux gathering at Bear Butte (near present Sturgis, South Dakota) had just concluded, and the three bands traveled down to hunt buffalo together. Discovering Warren's men, the Sioux were furious. Some wanted to kill the whites, though they knew any disturbance would stampede thousands of buffalo nearby.

Two uneasy, uncomfortable days passed as a snow and sleet storm blew in. The young Sioux guide hired at Fort Laramie deserted to join friends in the Minneconjou camp. Finally it was decided that Warren and his men should wait three days to meet with the Hunkpapa chief, Bear's Rib, arbitrarily appointed "first chief" by an earlier treaty commission.

When the chief did not appear, Warren's men backtracked about forty miles, then proceeded east. Chief Bear's Rib and another Indian overtook them, warning them to go no farther. But after one full day's deliberation, Bear's Rib agreed to ride with them part way, for safety. In exchange he asked Lieutenant Warren to tell the President and the white people that they could not be allowed into this country, adding that the Sioux people wished to be left alone. Despite what the peace treaty said, Bear's Rib vowed that they would continue to fight their old enemies, the Crows.

The Warren Expedition completed its reconnaissance of the eastern portion of the Black Hills but saw no more Indians.

In his report, Warren wrote sympathetically of the Sioux hunters, comparing their "feelings for us (as) not unlike what we should feel toward a person who should insist on setting fires to our barns." During the party's delay at Inyan Kara Mountain, he noted that the peak "is basaltic, and the appearance through a powerful spy-glass of those to the north, known as Bear Lodge and the Little Missouri Buttes, indicates that they are also of this formation."

Though Lieutenant Warren recommended further exploration —beyond the Big Horn Mountains and into the Upper Yellowstone and Powder River country—he was not to be part of such an undertaking. He was transferred to West Point the summer of 1859, and a newcomer to the west, Captain William F. Raynolds, headed the Yellowstone Expedition of that year.

Larger and more elaborate than Warren's party, the Yellowstone Expedition was guided by Jim Bridger and again included geologist F. V. Hayden, topographers, meteorologists, an artist, several civilians and a thirty-man military escort.

Its purpose was to obtain additional information about the Indians, record climatological data and catalog mineral resources as well as to search out several wagon routes over a wide area: a route from Fort Laramie to the Yellowstone, another north along the base of the Big Horns, one from Yellowstone to South Pass and a fourth between sources of the Wind River and Missouri tributaries.

On June 28, they headed west from Fort Pierre, Dakota Territory. Water was brackish, and the scorching sun blistered the men's lips. Temperatures averaged 100°–110°. Raynolds declared the whole country unfit for habitation. But farther west the terrain leveled out as they approached the northern rim of the Black Hills. For four days the bulky profile of Bear Butte wavered before them on the horizon. Inside the mountain, Sioux legend said, a huge wounded bear sat pouting, licking its wounds, defeated in battle by a dinosaur back in the sunrise of time.

Temperatures lowered. On July 11, the men camped a mile below Bear Butte. After dinner a party of men climbed to the top.

It had rained throughout the afternoon but just before sundown the rain let up and sun burned through the heavy overcast. A beautiful rainbow spanned the butte in front of their camp. Raynolds wrote: "The mountain was very nearly in the centre of the arch, clothed in delicate purple tints, the contrast with the dark clouds in the background forming a scene of singular beauty."

It seemed a good omen, the rainbow over Bear Butte, though perhaps only the Sioux guide knew the mountain was held sacred by Cheyenne and Sioux people, the site of vision quests for centuries.

Steady rain throughout the next day's march dampened the new recruits' spirits as well as their uniforms. Many Indian signs and abandoned camps were seen, as well as a Sun Dance lodge. July 15 Raynolds noted that their campsite was marked by the remains of an immense Indian lodge, "the frame of which consists of poles over thirty feet in length." Close by was a high post, ringing it a circle of buffalo skulls.

Other dated entries from Raynolds daily logs follow.

July 18: "Before us is the valley of two rivers: that of the *chan-cho-ka-wah-pa,* or thick-timbered river, known as the Little Missouri . . . in another direction, the valley of the north fork of the Shayenne (earlier spelling and name of the Belle Fourche River). Far in the distance, up the valley . . . the eye also notices the singular peak of Bear Lodge, rising like an enormous tower, and, from its resemblance to an Indian lodge, suggesting the origin of its title."

On July 19 at 4 A.M. pick and shovel details began to level the river banks so that the wagons could cross. After several hours the column moved out, laboriously crossing many sagebrush-filled gullies. A party of five men started toward Bear Lodge, but returned "without any positive conviction they had seen it."

Small herds of buffalo grazed here in this rugged, broken country and much of the grass had been eaten away. Jim Bridger and several of the soldiers killed three buffalo cows. A pack of wolves was seen in the distance, running down a buffalo calf. Just as the column rounded a ridge, three large bulls charged at the wagon train. A panicky trooper yelled, "Elephants! Elephants! My God, I didn't know there were elephants in this country." One of the mule teams bolted and was checked with great difficulty. Raynolds called it "probably the first buffalo chase on record with a six mule team."

The next day, July 20, Mr. Hutton, the topographer, and the Sioux guide, Zephyr Recontre, made a second attempt to reach Bear Lodge. "They returned to camp about 3 P.M. and report having found it . . . an isolated rock upon the bank of the river,

This map shows portions of the Yellowstone and Missouri tributaries, as explored by the expedition guided by Captain W. F. Raynolds, Topographical Engineer, and Lieutenant H. E. Maynadier in 1859–60. It was drawn to accompany the geological report of F. V. Hayden. Note that Devils Tower was still designated ''Bear Lodge.'' *(National Park Service)*

striking . . . from the fact it rises from a valley, but by no means forming a prominent landmark when viewed from the north.''

That day, the Missouri Buttes, higher than Bear Lodge, were visible ahead. Raynolds wrote that about an hour after the train moved on, the Indian guide was missing. ''When last noticed he was looking for a point at which to cross the gully, and having found one, uttered his usual cry, *washte* (good) and then sought shelter from a slight shower under a neighboring pine. He remained there until the train had passed, and then quietly slipped away.''

For several nights the men uneasily observed night fires, flickering in the distance near Bear Lodge. Raynolds assumed that since they were entering Crow territory, perhaps Zephyr Recontre did not want to go farther. He wrote in praise of the Indian's skill as a guide, his good temper and knowledge of the country they traveled over.

Hayden's detailed geological report, included in Raynolds' material, identified terrain and rock strata and mentioned ''very decided evidence of the existence of gold.'' But not for fifteen years would another government expedition intrude on Indian lands. Following the Civil War, pressures accelerated in both Washington and in the West to open up the country that lay north of the North Platte River.

On July 25, 1868, even while residents of the new commonwealth—Wyoming Territory—were celebrating and shooting off fireworks, scouts were searching the Big Horn Mountains to bring in Red Cloud—*Mahpiya Luta*, great warrior and Oglala chief—and his people from their prime hunting grounds, to sign the treaty which was underway.

Only a few months later Territorial Secretary Edward M. Lee informed the first Wyoming Legislature that there was gold in the Big Horns and the Black Hills, adding that development of gold fields was slowed down by Indian occupancy, but stating that movements were underway to open up one of the richest gold regions ever to be discovered.

This treaty which was to end the bloody Indian-white conflict

More than a thousand men with Brevet Major General George Armstrong Custer's Expedition explored the interior of the Black Hills for two months in 1874. Included were three companies of infantry, a marching band, glee club and sixty Indian scouts as well as scientists, newspaper reporters, miners and photographers. Heavy overcast obscured their view toward Bear Lodge and the Missouri Buttes, however. *(National Archives Photo no. 77-HQ-264-854 [Illingsworth Collection])*

on the northern plains, establish reservations and agencies and set aside unceded lands, also prevented the Indians from crossing the North Platte River to trade at Fort Laramie. There was heavy white traffic now along the Oregon Trail between Fort Laramie and Red Buttes (near present Casper), some of it north of the North Platte.

By the late 1860s and early 1870s, an estimated twenty thousand tribal people were living in the Powder River Basin-Black Hills area of Wyoming and South Dakota, and in southern Wyoming and the South Pass gold mining districts to the west, about half that many whites. With completion of the transcontinental railroad, more and more settlers were pushing west.

Confusion surrounding treaty provisions dealing with farming and, more important, interpretation of boundaries took Red Cloud and other Sioux leaders to meet with officials in Washington in 1870.

In 1873 a financial panic, the worst in the nation's history, swept the country. Taxes were high and the public debt was enormous. Several eastern banks failed and the stock exchange closed for ten days.

Back in Wyoming Territory, cattlemen were eager to push their herds north to the rich grass.

In July, 1874, Brevet Major General George Armstrong Custer's Seventh Cavalry, two companies of infantry with a Gatling gun, marching band and glee club and sixty Indian scouts—more than a thousand men, including scientists, newspapermen, a photographer and some miners—scouted the interior of the Black Hills for sixty days.

Entering a corner of Montana Territory, they swung down through northeastern Wyoming. Custer and several others climbed Inyan Kara Mountain, where seventeen years earlier Sioux buffalo hunters had halted the Warren expedition. One of the officers carved "Custer '74" into the rock, but heavy overcast obscured the view toward Bear Lodge and the Missouri Buttes. Or had the Sioux again set fire to the grass? Gold from the grass roots down was the report that circulated nationwide. "*Pahuska* (Long Hair, or Custer) had told about it with a voice that went everywhere,'' said Black Elk, Sioux holy man.

The next year brought many changes. During May and June of 1875, while Red Cloud, Spotted Tail (*Sinte Gleska*, chief of the Brule Sioux) and other Sioux chiefs met in Washington with government officials to discuss the sale or lease of mineral rights, miners and surveyors with the government-sponsored Newton-Jenney Expedition looked for gold in the Black Hills. Washington peace commissioners came west to visit various agencies to arrange a grand council, escorted by a dozen of Red Cloud's and Spotted Tail's best warriors, and found surveyors staking claims. The Hills were full of miners, many already taking out large quantities of gold. Troops ordered to expel all whites from these Indian lands were peacefully camped near the miners.

Conflicting estimates of gold discovered during the Custer Expedition led to the War Department's authorization of the Newton-Jenney Expedition. Heading it was Walter P. Jenney, assisted by Henry Newton, both of the Columbia School of Mines in New York.

Besides the two geologists, the sixteen-man scientific party included an astronomer, engineer, topographical assistant, a botanist and a crew of miners and laborers.

Prepared for a long five months in the field, Colonel Richard I. Dodge commanded the military escort of more than four hundred men: infantrymen, six companies of cavalry, assorted teamsters, wagonmasters, packers, a guide, butcher, civilian herders, 397 mules and over 130 beef cattle.

On May 25, the column pulled out of Fort Laramie, arriving nine days later at a spot named Camp Jenney, in Wyoming, just south of present Newcastle. The pack train unloaded, and construction of a storehouse was begun. The scientific party separated into two groups, Jenney's party to investigate mineral resources, primarily gold, and Newton's group to conduct topographical studies.

Dodge's journal for June 6 notes that the storehouse was finished, and scouts and exploring parties sent out. Indians were

The War Department in 1875 authorized geologists Henry Newton (shown) and Walter P. Jenney to explore the Black Hills for gold. Newton recorded the first detailed description of Bear Lodge and the Missouri Buttes. During the Newton-Jenney Expedition, Bear Lodge became known on maps as Devils Tower. *(South Dakota State Historical Society)*

seen nearby, but none approached them. The pack train returned
to Fort Laramie for supplies, taking the mail out. From this central
storehouse and stockade, supplies would go out to a series of
base camps established throughout the Hills, he wrote.

But interesting anecdotes and daily details of camp life, military
movements and difficulties encountered in making fifteen hundred
miles of wagon road and more than six thousand miles of horseback trail over rough terrain are missing from his journal.

Walter Jenney, however, sent out a number of letters which
circulated widely, some appearing in the *Cheyenne Daily Leader*
in June and July. His final report, described as "cautious," was
favorable concerning the presence of gold in paying quantities.
Yet rumors spread that he had discovered an incredibly rich placer
mine, and the *Yankton Daily Press & Dakotaian* headline predicted "Dakota Mines to Eclipse the World." "Gold Enough to
Pay the National Debt" declared the *Bismarck Tribune*.

Jenney's last dispatch to the Commissioner of Indian Affairs,
dated October 11, 1875—less than a week before he returned to
Fort Laramie—related "gold in small quantities in the Bear Lodge
Mountains about twenty miles east of the Little Missouri
Buttes . . ."

Henry Newton's report described both Bear Lodge and the
Missouri Buttes as seen from the west, noting that they "appear
in line . . . the former resembling in appearance the huge stump
of a tree, its surface striated vertically from top to base, and,
being perched on the crest of a high, flat-topped ridge, it becomes
a very prominent landmark . . . once seen, so singular and unique
that it can never be forgotten."

His excitement in seeing the tower close up is evident. He
wrote that Bear Lodge "was not reached by the Warren Expedition, but while the Raynolds Expedition was in the vicinity of
the Little Missouri River, two attempts, the last successful, were
made by Mr. Hutton to reach it. He recorded no particular description of it, so that when we reached it . . . our examination
had all the charm of novelty. Its remarkable structure, its sym-
metry and its prominence make it an unfailing object of

Shown is one of a group of 40 stereopticon photos taken during the Newton-Jenney Expedition of 1875. Exhibited at the St. Louis Fair in 1876, the photos received first prize for the best photographic exhibit. *(Jennewein Collection, Dakota Wesleyan University)*

wonder . . . Its summit is so entirely inaccessible that the energetic explorer . . . standing at its base could only look upward in despair of ever planting his feet on top.''

Newton also added that the name "Bear Lodge" appears on the earliest maps, but that it is "more recently known among the Indians as 'the bad god's tower', or, in better English, 'the devil's tower.' ''[1]

So it would be known on maps, ever after.

But Devils Tower's "inaccessible" top would not remain so for long.

[1]Among the papers in the Dick Stone manuscript is an undated letter from hereditary Oglala Sioux chief Luther Standing Bear concerning the name change. (Standing Bear, born about 1868, wrote several books, including *My People the Sioux* and *Land of the Spotted Eagle,* published during the late 1920s and early 1930s, and still considered standard works about Sioux life and culture.) His letter states that "Colonel Dodge was, as were so many white men in meddling with Indian history, wrong in saying the Indians called the place 'the bad god's tower.' The Sioux had no word for devil, for the devil and hades of the white man had no place in Indian thought." Colonel Dodge's book, *The Black Hills,* previously cited, includes the same information about Indians referring to the "bad god's tower." Perhaps due to Henry Newton's untimely death in Deadwood, South Dakota, on August 5, 1877, when he returned for further information about the Black Hills, Colonel Dodge is the one most often given credit—or blame—for renaming the tower. Another objection to the name change was registered by H. L. Scott, Major General, Retired, in a letter he wrote in 1920 to the president of the Wyoming Historical Society, now retained at Cheyenne at the Wyoming State Archives, Museums and Historical Department. Scott's letter said, in part, that he was "outraged that Colonel Dodge should so violate a precedent of explorer's ethics as to change the name . . . to Devils Tower, a name without taste, meaning or historical precedent—which received its vogue because there were no white people in the country when Warren and Raynolds made their reports but were coming in when Dodge wrote his work, which was so much sought after by newcomers." Author of a number of articles about Indian life, Scott graduated from West Point only a few days before the Custer battle. He applied for duty with the Seventh Cavalry. As a Second Lieutenant in the Dakotas, Montana and northern Wyoming area, he became deeply interested in Indian life, history and culture, eventually becoming expert at sign language and participating in a number of tribal ceremonies among the Sioux, Cheyenne and Arapaho. Stationed at Fort Sill, Oklahoma, he was later to serve as Adjutant General to the Military Governor of Cuba during the war with Spain. Scott later served as Superintendent of West Point.

Works Cited

Information regarding the Warren Expedition is taken from the original report. See G. K. Warren's *Preliminary Report* (35th Congress, 2d sess., 24 November 1858). An interesting overview of western exploration can be found in William H. Goetzmann's *Army Exploration in the American West: 1803–1863* (New Haven: Yale University, 1959). See also George E. Hyde's *Red Cloud's Folk* (Norman: University of Oklahoma, 1937). An interesting, detailed report of his expedition is W. F. Raynolds' *Report on the Exploration of the Yellowstone and the Country Drained by That River* (40th Congress, 1st sess., 19 July 1867). Additional background material can be found in N. A. Higginbotham's "Wind-Roan Bear Winter Count," *Plains Anthropologist* 26, no. 91 (1981); Agnes Wright Spring's *Cheyenne and Black Hills Stage Routes* (Glendale: University of Nebraska, Bison Books, 1972); the previously cited *Archeology of the Eastern Powder River Basin*; and T. A. Larson's *History of Wyoming*, 2 ed. rev. (Lincoln: University of Nebraska, 1978). Additional Treaty of 1868 information is contained in a study by Raymond J. DeMallie, Jr., "Treaties Made Between Nations," *The Great Sioux Nation: Sitting In Judgment on America,* edited by Roxanne Dunbar Ortiz (Berkeley: Moon Books, Inc., 1977). For some background on the Custer expedition see Donald Jackson's *Custer's Gold: The United States Cavalry Expedition of 1874* (Lincoln: University of Nebraska, Bison Books, 1966). Specifics of the Newton-Jenney expedition can be found in Lesta V. Turchen and James D. McLaird's *The Black Hills Expedition of 1875* (Mitchell: Dakota Wesleyan Press, 1975). See also Walter Jenney's *The Mineral Wealth, Climate and Rainfall and Natural Resources of the Black Hills of Dakota*, Senate Exec. Doc. 51 (44th Cong., 1st sess. Washington: U.S. Government Printing Office, 1875–76). and Henry Newton's remarks contained in T. A. Jagger's *Laccoliths of the Black Hills Area, South Dakota and Wyoming* (Washington: Government Printing Office, 1901).

Classic Climbs

Less than twenty years after surveyors declared Devils Tower "inaccessible to anything without wings," a Wyoming rancher proved them wrong.

"I'll be up on top of Devils Tower before three years," boasted Will Rogers to his brother-in-law, in 1890.

He had heard it before. "Yes, and you'll break your neck, too, Will," he said.

"No, I won't," insisted Rogers, "but I'll be up there."

William B. Rogers, a large, raw-boned man—called Will or Bill—didn't fear man or the devil, according to his sister.

A miner who came to the Black Hills in 1878 after the gold rush peaked, Rogers drifted into Wyoming in the early 1880s when Crook County had fewer than 250 people. He worked a while at the Shipwheel Ranch. Then he and young Wayne Morris bought a wagon and harness. They wintered in a dugout with a canvas door. When food ran low they hauled buffalo meat and deer hides to Deadwood, South Dakota, and sold them. Eventually they built a cabin and ran their own cattle.

In 1886, the partnership broke up. Already over thirty years old, Rogers met and married twenty-two year old Linnie Knowles. Morris kept the ranch, and Rogers and his new wife moved the cattle to a new homestead in sight of Devils Tower.

By now the tower was a favorite camping spot; its grassy meadows and cold springs near the base attracted many visitors.

Before the bridge was constructed, early visitors at the tower arrived by horseback and in wagons, sometimes having to ford the swollen Belle Fourche River seven or eight times to reach the base of Devils Tower. *(Wyoming State Archives, Museums and Historical Department)*

Enduring the rugged, roadless approach, fording the meandering Belle Fourche River seven or eight times, even risking being stranded by flash floods was considered worth the trip. Though large cattle outfits such as MacKenzie's Campstool and the 101 controlled land in the area, a number of smaller homesteads were also being established.

But in February 1890, when a Charles Graham filed to obtain ownership of the land under Devils Tower, the General Land Office rejected the application. That summer Wyoming became a state. Crook County had more than two thousand people. Local support grew to designate the tower and the Missouri Buttes either

Professional wolf hunters in the 1890s took hundreds of gray wolf pelts in the Devils Tower area. *(Wyoming State Archives, Museums and Historical Department)*

a state park or a national park. In March 1891, a temporary forest reserve of some sixty square miles was created.[1]

New neighbors of the Rogers' in 1893 were the Ripleys: Alice Mae, 19, known as Dollie, and her twenty-eight-year-old husband, Willard. They dreamed of expanding their ranch on the Belle Fourche River, about two miles north of Devils Tower, but it wouldn't be easy.

Times were hard. A nationwide depression was on. Farm prices plunged, and strikes and widespread unemployment plagued the east. Banks failed. Several in Wyoming had already closed their doors. To Colonel Ripley, Willard's father, who was then in his late fifties—a former postmaster, store owner and hotel proprietor—promoting Rogers' Devils Tower climb seemed like a real money maker.

The Fourth of July would be the best time to draw a crowd, he decided. The women could run a food stand. But one pressing problem would be figuring out just how Bill Rogers was going to get up there.

For several weeks that spring the men experimented with kites, trying to fly one over the tower and eventually attach a permanent rope to the top, but the kites wouldn't fly high enough. When one kite lodged in a crevice, they began to consider the possibility of wedging stakes into cracks and building a ladder. Rogers scanned the tower with field glasses. Eventually he located a long, continuous crack on the southeast side.

As Dollie Ripley told it to Dick Stone, it was late April when Bill Rogers and the Colonel began cutting oak, ash and willow trees. Sawing them into two-and-a-half-foot lengths about three inches in diameter, they hauled the pegs by wagon a quarter of a mile to the tower base. From there they climbed the talus slope to the rope and pulley Willard had rigged up. He would do most of the actual building.

---

[1] This acreage was reduced to about eighteen square miles the following year. Wyoming Senator Francis E. Warren introduced a bill in the U.S. Senate for the establishment of Devils Tower National Park, also. The bill was read twice, referred to committee, but Congress took no action.

A miner and rancher, William B. Rogers boasted in 1890 that he would stand on the tower top within three years. In 1893 he did just that, by means of a wooden ladder. *(Wyoming State Archives, Museums and Historical Department)*

Oak, ash and willow limbs were sawed into two-and-a-half-foot pegs and hauled to the base of Devils Tower. There Willard Ripley (shown) and his father, Colonel Ripley, had rigged up a rope and pulley system allowing Willard to wedge in pegs to build the ladder. Construction took several months. *(National Park Service)*

Because Willard was left handed, he could better manipulate the hammer from some angles. As he balanced on a section of ladder just completed, he reached up to drive in the next four or five pegs. Then he sawed these pieces off evenly and nailed a piece of two-by-four along the outer edge.

Dollie Ripley waited alone in camp, cooking for the men. From the ground, dwarfed by the immense rise of rock, Willard looked smaller and smaller, the growing ladder a child's construction. Several times high wind and afternoon heat radiating off the rock face forced him down. She knew that building the ladder was hard, dangerous work—more dangerous, maybe, than the exhibition climb would be.

As the long crack narrowed higher up, Willard hammered in pegs about two inches in diameter. Part way above the narrower section, the crack ran at a different angle. The building, as well as the climbing, would have to be accomplished from the opposite side because of a bulging column.

While Willard was finishing the ladder, Bill Rogers attended to other details. By now a number of others were also involved in the coming celebration. Handbills were printed up and circulated, by order of a Crook County Committee, advertising "the rarest sight of a lifetime" and declaring that "the 4th of July will be better spent at the Devils Tower than at the World's Fair. Old Glory will be flung to the breeze from the top of the tower by Wm. Rogers."

Hay and grain to be furnished for the horses was hauled in. Dollie Ripley and Linnie Rogers went after flour and other supplies for bread they would bake to serve with the roast meat. Two prominent lawyers were invited to speak.

Some ladies from Deadwood, South Dakota, brought Rogers a handsewn Uncle Sam suit. In mid-June, not knowing where to send for a twelve-by-seven foot flag, Rogers asked a Sundance artist, Truman Fox, to make one. Fox sewed strips of muslin together, painted on red stripes and filled in the blue field for the forty-four stars. Rogers rode horseback to Sundance to pick it up.

On June 29, the ladder was finished, its top about two hundred feet below the summit of Devils Tower. Now came the tricky part.

To leave the top of the ladder Rogers would have to stand on the topmost rung, stretch up to "belly over" the top of a column where there was a foothold, then work upward along an insloping, rocky shoulder for a hundred feet. The final hundred-foot scramble was an easier climb over deep cracks and boulders.

But which of the two men first reached the tower top to secure the two-hundred-foot fixed rope? Was it Willard Ripley because he nailed together most of the ladder or Bill Rogers whose long dream it was to be the first man to stand on Devils Tower? No one is sure.

By July 3, many people had already arrived and more were coming. The Deadwood stage came with a full load of passengers. Three unidentified men climbed the ladder, packing up sections of the flagpole. Wyoming families from the Sundance, Beulah and Minnesela communities visited with old and new South Dakota friends from Deadwood, Lead, Central, Terraville, Rapid City, Sturgis, Spearfish and Belle Fourche. By evening between seven hundred and eight hundred people were camped on the north side of the tower and along the Belle Fourche River. During the night a light rain fell.

July 4 dawned clear and sunny. The main speakers didn't arrive, so about 9 A.M. two ministers in the crowd delivered spontaneous orations. A young boy gave a recitation entitled "America," and a volunteer choir sang. Will Rogers was presented with the flag and the suit he would wear.

About ten o'clock, wearing his white jacket with red emblem and the blue pants, Rogers began the historic climb. Men passed around field glasses. About noon when his tiny figure was sighted, arms waving, a cheer rose from the crowd. The flag snapped in the stiff breeze, the sound audible below. Will Rogers, forty years old, had done it.

As he climbed down, he heard fiddle and organ music. Dancing began on the wooden platform. Horseshoes and other games

DEVIL'S TOWER

GREATEST NATURAL WONDERS ~~~ UNITED STATES.

Situated in

CROOK COUNTY, WYOMING.

The Devil's Tower is a perpendicular column of rock and no human being has ever stepped upon its top.

On July 4th, 1893, Old Glory will be flung to the breeze from the top of the Tower, 800 feet from the ground by Wm. Rogers.

The Committee of citizens of Crook County have organized the following programme:

○ SPEAKERS: ○

Hon. N. K. Griggs, Beatrice, Neb.
Col. Wm. R. Steele, Deadwood, So. Dak.
Presentation of costume to Mr. Rogers by ladies of Deadwood, So. Dak.

Presentation of Flag to be floated on the Tower by ladies of Spearfish, So. Dak.

○ Marshal of the Day: ○
E. B. Armstrong, Sheriff Crook County.

Aids to Marshal:

Chas. Williams,	Hulett.
Harry Stevens,	Barrett.
John Mahnken,	Bochin.
Ed. Ludlow,	Beulah.
Wm. H. Southerland,	Riverdale.
Emil Krouse,	Inyan Kara.
Mead Fish,	Black Buttes.
R. Williams,	Williams Divide.
E. L. Burke,	Tower.
Ed. Fitch,	Gillett.
Leroy Salisbury,	Linden.
Tom Nefsy,	Linden.
A. S. Bender,	Alva.

THERE WILL BE PLENTY TO EAT AND DRINK ON THE GROUNDS

LOTS OF HAY AND GRAIN FOR HORSES.

Dancing day and Night.

Perfect order will be maintained. The rarest sight of a lifetime will be observed, and the 4th of July will be better spent at the Devil's Tower than at the World's Fair.

BY ORDER OF Crook County Committee.

''Perfect order will be maintained'' declared the handbill advertising Rogers's Fourth of July Devils Tower climb, with dancing day and night and hay for the horses. *(Wyoming State Archives, Museums and Historical Department)*

At left is Newell Joyner, Custodian at Devils Tower from 1932–47, and area resident George Grenier, posed below remains of the Rogers-Ripley ladder which was built in 1893. *(National Park Service)*

Linnie and Will Rogers and their daughter were Crook County residents. In 1895, Rogers persuaded his wife to do a solo climb up Devils Tower. *(National Park Service)*

entertained the younger children. The food stands sold out.

Time and again that afternoon Rogers repeated that no, there wasn't really much up there on top—a few crevices with dirt and greasewood caught in them, grass and cedar bushes, lots of loose rock. Some eye witnesses said several other men also went up the ladder later on that day. Another said there was nothing to the report that a twelve-year-old boy climbed up and sat dangling his legs over the edge and almost fell.

In mid-afternoon the wind picked up, blowing the flag down onto the dance platform. It was cut up and sold for souvenirs. The Rogers' share of souvenir sales and food stand proceeds that day were said to have totaled nearly five hundred dollars.

Two years later Rogers somehow convinced his thirty-one-year-old wife to make a second exhibition climb.

He nailed together a ladder and braced it against a tall pine tree near their home. Day by day he inclined it more steeply until she could climb almost straight up. Then he took her to Devils Tower to practice.

He tied a rope around her waist, and climbing ahead of her, half-hitched or belayed the rope around a rung of the ladder. As she climbed toward him he took up the slack. The couple made three practice climbs. Will fixed ropes in several dangerous places in preparation for the solo climb. On July 4, 1895, Linnie Rogers—wearing knee-high leather boots and a specially designed navy blue bloomer suit with wide sleeves—became the first woman to stand on Devils Tower.[2]

Over a period of years, a number of people probably climbed the ladder. No doubt some went only part way, backing down rather than risking the leap from the security of the top rung to go the last two hundred feet. The summer of 1903 two members of the Geological Survey camped at the tower base and climbed ''with much difficulty'' because some wooden pegs were missing and others were dangerously loose.

In 1927, Babe White, ''The Human Fly,'' announced plans to scale the rock face barehanded, without artificial devices, ''like a squirrel going up a tree.'' Sketchy reports from the *Sundance Times* and the *Colony* (Wyoming) *Coyote* chronicled his story.

While in Denver in mid-August completing arrangements to climb the Midland Savings Bank Building, White and his manager made a fast trip to Sundance and the Devils Tower area.

In early September his advance man, Jack Wilson, returned alone to generate publicity. In Sundance Wilson showed movies

---

[2]Linnie Rogers' record apparently stood for fifty-three years. In 1948, Jan Conn, climbing with her husband Herb, became the first woman to ascend with modern climbing equipment. Three years later, she and Jan Showacre made the first two-woman ascent of Devils Tower. A number of other women have climbed since then.

of White climbing a Mexico City cathedral before thousands of people. White had walked a high wire twenty stories up, at one point lying down on his back on the wire. Wilson told *Times* reporters that White was the most daring "human fly" in the business and claimed he had climbed every important building in the world.

White's Devils Tower climb was to be the highlight of the Crook County Fair on September 11.

The *Colony Coyote* noted that while headquartered in Sundance, Babe White suffered an embarrassing mishap. Attempting to mount a twelve-foot ladder in the belfry of the Sundance courthouse, he slipped, severely bruising his leg which had to be bandaged—perhaps a harbinger of things to come.

Promising to perform a number of stunts during the climb, the "Human Fly" stated he would return the one dollar per head fee if he were unable to reach the tower top.

According to the *Colony Coyote,* the White climb was both disappointing and disgusting. That paper reported White climbed the tower with the aid of pegs and rope ladders which he had previously rigged up. But the *Times* stated he used the old Rogers-Ripley ladder on the lower level, though the top two hundred feet were "human flied." The only thrilling moments were when White at first couldn't find the top of the ladder and, later, when one of the pegs gave way underfoot during his descent.

At Babe White's recommendation, the National Park Service removed the lower portion of the ladder. In 1972, the top 160 feet were restored as a historic feature of Devils Tower.

For a number of years during the Depression, Devils Tower was considered "unclimbable," except by some artificial means such as a ladder. In 1934, the editor of a climbing journal, *Appalachia,* wrote that climbing it seemed out of the question. "The walls are without holds save for narrow cracks, and the angles and distances between columns are far too wide to admit to chimney techniques . . ." (bracing the back against one wall and the feet against the other and working upward.)

In 1927, Babe White, a circus aerialist and performer, arrived in Sundance and announced plans to climb Devils Tower during the Crook County Fair in September. He planned to climb ''barehanded and without artificial devices.'' *(Photo from the author's collection)*

Although mountain climbing was beginning to catch on in the United States at private eastern clubs and in groups associated with Harvard, Yale and Dartmouth Universities, European climbing was far more advanced. Among the excellent Italian and German climbers were those who felt that had Devils Tower been located in the eastern Alps, it would have been scaled by legitimate means well before 1900.

German-born Fritz Wiessner had heard about Wyoming's tower. At sixteen he had led climbers up sandstone towers near his home in Dresden; later, to the rock walls of the Dolomites in northeastern Italy and Austria; eventually, to Nanga Parbat in the Himalayas, at twenty-six thousand feet the sixth highest mountain in the world.

In September 1936, after climbing in British Columbia and in the Tetons, Wiessner and several companions returning to New York swung over to check out the "unclimbable" shaft.

After studying the tower intently for about thirty minutes, he stated it could be climbed. Though Devils Tower Custodian Newell Joyner received them cordially and telephoned Washington for permission for the climb, it was refused. But the following summer Wiessner's application did go through. Climbing with him would be Bill House and Lawrence Coveney.

Unlike the Rogers-Ripley event, this climb would be in no way an exhibition. The climbers were coming at their own expense. They requested no publicity.

With field glasses Wiessner chose the route the afternoon of June 26. The others also studied it, the key to the climb being several uneven columns on the southeast corner, about 250 feet south of the remains of the wood ladder. These columns which broke the sheer, upward sweep of the sides, varied from six to eight feet in diameter and were rounded off, appearing nearly cylindrical. Unlike most of the columns on the tower which lay close to the rock behind them, these stair-step columns were set out, six to twelve inches from the rock face. Wiessner's team thought it might be possible to climb up these cracks to reach the column tops.

Ropes and equipment were laid out the night before. The climb was set for 6:30 A.M., June 27. That morning as they scrambled several hundred feet above the talus slope, the first problem confronted them—a stubborn gooseberry bush which nearly prevented them from reaching a higher ledge. They formed a three man stand, with Wiessner climbing to stand on House's shoulders and tearing the bush out with his leather gloves.

The bush conquered, the others joined Wiessner on the ledge. The three were roped together with 125 feet of rope, though each man would do his own climbing. The rope served only as protection in the event of a fall. Only one man at a time would ascend.

All three men carried pitons, steel pins varying in size from two to six inches long with an open eye, which could be driven into the rock with a small hammer. If necessary, before a difficult area, a piton could be driven into the rock and the rope clipped into the eye of the piton with a carabiner, an oval-shaped clip. This would anchor the rope closer to an ascending climber, thus shortening a possible fall.

With the rope around his waist and secured to a point behind him, Wiessner belayed Coveney up. Keeping the rope taut and out of Coveney's way by anticipating his moves, Wiessner paid out the rope with one hand and took up the slack with the other. Coveney belayed House. One eighteen and another twenty foot climb brought them to the base of the first column.

By now a few tourists had joined the Park Service personnel and other spectators below them. Fragments of conversation drifted up. They heard a woman say, "Oh, he's pulling the man up now."

Ascending higher as Coveney and House waited, Wiessner reported that the long crack leading up to the tallest column looked good. They joined him on the platform. House wrote, in *American Alpine Journal*: "To the right, separated from our platform by a gap of six feet, lay the most evil looking crack I have ever seen. For eighty feet it went up practically without a break in its smooth edges. One side was the wall of rock—the other, the rounded corner of the columns. The crack was vertical and varied from six to nine inches in width . . . We had to admit what we feared the night before—that if this crack would not go, we would be unable to reach the top.''

This was the steepest part of Devils Tower. By now, mid-morning heat was increasing, and the climbers realized sunstroke was a possibility.

In Lawrence Coveney's account in *Appalachia* he noted they were not optimistic at this point as he ''mentally rehearsed the rope handling which would work best in case of a fall. Bill put himself in position to anchor me. Fritz decided to climb with a double rope. He was determined but very tense. In the crack, Fritz climbed at first with effort, but after some fifteen feet all seemed well. A shoulder and elbow, thrust into the crack, provided the friction hold which enabled him to raise a knee. By a turn of the ankle, sufficient pressure was maintained with heel, toe and knee to straighten the body upward and again jam his shoulder and arm in the crack a few inches higher.

''He was now climbing rhythmically with his characteristic flawless technique . . . A bulge in the edge of the column forced his shoulders back but did not delay him more than a minute . . . We knew we were watching an exhibition such as few climbers ever see. A one inch ledge gave Fritz a chance to pause and a quick survey disclosed a small crack on the wall. A piton (the only one used in the ascent) was driven in and we felt much better with the thought that a fall would be broken above instead of forty to eighty feet below the belay man . . . It was now a question of endurance . . .''

His heels disappeared over the column and they heard Wiessner give a ''weird howl'' that meant they could go all the way.

As Wiessner prepared to belay the others, Coveney noted that ''both Bill and I were saved by the rope at the bulge (of the column). A short distance higher I was obliged to call for aid a second time. When I reached the top of the column it was plain that I would be in no position to belay Bill for several minutes and Fritz shouldered the duty . . . rather than lose time.''

The hardest climbing was now behind them. An irregular,

Left to right: Bill House, Lawrence Coveney, Fritz Wiessner. German-born Fritz Wiessner, an experienced world climber in Europe and the Himalayas, led the first alpine climbing team up Devils Tower. He requested that the Park Service release no publicity. On top of the tower, the three climbers found remnants of the flagpole Will Rogers had planted there fifty-six years previously. *(National Park Service)*

hundred-foot chimney which they could work into led to the wide, sloping shoulder that extends almost the entire width of the east wall. Here they unroped, rested a few minutes and easily walked up the remaining two hundred feet. At 11:18 they stood on top.

Unable to eat their sandwiches, they ate oranges and shared a can of grapefruit juice, commenting—as Bill Rogers had in 1893—on the unimpressive top of the tower. Bill House, a forestry major, gathered samples of each variety of cactus, grass and weed he found growing. They saw several crickets and a chipmunk. As a joke, Coveney and House diverted Wiessner's attention and shot off some firecrackers.

By now the direct rays of the sun were almost unbearably hot. Quickly they built a large cairn, leaving their names and the date there inside the juice can. A little before noon, they began the series of six rappels—slides down the rope—which would take them down to the bottom. Wiessner drove in a piton. Facing the tower, he straddled the rope, then pulled it behind him and over his head to the opposite shoulder.

Farther down, nervous tension, heat and muscular strain began to tell. Coveney wrote: "We were standing on the top of the high column when Fritz rappeled, and watching (the piton) intently when it began to bend . . . it moved . . . Bill shouted a warning and seized the rope. I clutched Bill around the waist to give him support and after safe assurance from us, Fritz continued his descent. He insisted . . . that the piton would hold, and later observations showed that probably he was right. Nonetheless, Bill and I decided to drive in another piton and double the safety factor."

As the last of the three men rappeled to the ground about 1:30 P.M., the spectators cheered. Men from the nearby Civilian Conservation Corps camp met them with canteens of water. Tourists took pictures. In answer to a question, Lawrence Coveney explained that the rope was not used to lasso rock outcroppings overhead. Wiessner said that while he had made harder climbs of equal distance, this climb was hard and should not be attempted by amateurs. Bill House wrote later that it was not until that evening after they had found "much cold beer" that they began to feel human again.

Planning to repeat the Wiessner route up Devils Tower, Jack Durrance and a partner received permission to climb in September 1938.

Durrance, described as a free spirit given to singing German beer drinking songs and working out on the boulders near Jenny Lake Lodge at Jackson, Wyoming, had come to the state two years earlier to work for Paul Petzoldt who guided climbing parties up into the Tetons. Trained in the German climbing tradition, he had attended high school near Garmisch and worked in a Munich machine factory. A self-confident climber, he sought out the bare ridges and smooth walls in the Tetons, using pitons for security and exploring new routes. And he was eager to add Devils Tower to an impressive list of climbs.

Encountering the same, fierce gooseberry bush which had slowed down Wiessner's party, Durrance and his partner Harrison Butterworth reached the top of the second column when a sudden rain shower wet their ropes and made the tower sides dangerously slick. They climbed down, given permission by Custodian Joyner to spend the night in the basement of the ranger station.

At daybreak they returned, planning to ascend the same way, until Durrance noticed a possible route a few columns to the left of Wiessner's approach. Moving up past a broken column that tilted against a longer one, Durrance found the climbing here to be fairly easy. Disappearing into a short chimney, he emerged at the top of the column and belayed Butterworth.

Hard climbing was above them and Durrance double-roped for protection, taking a generous supply of pitons and working up the seventy-two foot crack. Soon the climbers stood on the column above what is now called the Durrance Crack. Above this were several short pitches and a traverse over into the low-angled, sloping area today's climbers call "The Meadows." From here it was an easy climb to the top.

Once up, they found the piton used in Fritz Wiessner's first rappel and a weatherbeaten stake they later learned was part of Will Rogers' flagstaff. Like the others, they found the tower top as unimpressive as any field of weeds and stones.

But Durrance had discovered a second, easier way to the top of Devils Tower. Until 1951, the Wiessner and Durrance routes were the only ways to ascend. The Durrance route is still the most popular of all routes today.

Three years after Jack Durrance first climbed the national monument, Park Service officials asked him to climb it again—this time to rescue a stranded man whose "media event" had failed.

Because most Devils Tower climbers ascend one specific area, Park Service officials believe their record of successful summit climbs is especially accurate. The Hopkins rescue accounts for the unusual number of climbers in 1941. The tower began receiving publicity from *Close Encounters of a Third Kind* in 1977.

SUCCESSFUL SUMMIT CLIMBS

Year	Parties	Climbers	Year	Parties	Climbers
1937	1	3	1967	51	134
1938	1	2	1968	53	136
1939	0	0	1969	71	184
1940	0	0	1970	82	216
1941	2	10	1971	103	297
1942	0	0	1972	138	357
1943	0	0	1973	121	312
1944	0	0	1974	164	424
1945	0	0	1975	183	494
1946	1	2	1976	308	774
1947	1	2	1977	445	1098
1948	2	18	1978	657	1638
1949	3	20	1979	805	1969
1950	1	2	1980	701	1754
1951	5	13	1981	667	1624
1952	7	19	1982	428	1277
1953	8	27	1983	617	1621
1954	12	42	1984	629	1266
1955	5	17	1985	648	1591
1956	53	158	1986	618	1477
1957	11	46	1987	627	1,596
1958	42	143	1988	671	1675
1959	32	119	1989	751	1879
1960	42	104	1990	682	1688
1961	50	123	1991	786	1694
1962	55	128	1992	816	2023
1963	36	92	1993	863	2166
1964	75	187	1994	879	2108
1965	48	119	**Total Parties**		**14,452**
1966	33	100	**Total Climbers**		**34,968**

Roped to climbers below him for safety, a modern climber ascends Devils Tower with an assortment of clips and carabiners. *(Photo by Tom Hough, courtesy of Elaine Hough)*

Park Service officials have kept records of non-summit climbs only since 1974

Non-Summit Climbs

Year	Climbers	Year	Climbers	Year	Climbers
1974	88	1981	1700	1988	4334
1975	117	1982	1753	1989	4283
1976	168	1983	1995	1990	3694
1977	183	1984	1870	1991	3727
1978	532	1985	2625	1992	4097
1979	659	1986	3301	1993	3409
1980	1053	1987	3303	1994	3927
		Total	**42,891**		

Works Cited

Details regarding the Rogers-Ripley ladder, the 1893 climb and Linnie Rogers' 1895 climb are taken from interviews and letters contained in Dick Stone's previously cited *History of Devils Tower,* as follows: Wayne Morris interview, September 23, 1934; Dollie Ripley interview, October 7, 1934; G. A. Knowles interview, n.d.; letter to Dick Stone from W. B. Ogden, October 16, 1934. See also *Pioneers of Crook County: 1876–1920* (Sundance: Crook County Historical Society, 1981); Nelson A. Bryant's *Pioneer Life in Northeastern Wyoming: From Smoke-Signals to Telstar* (Newton: Allen Publishing Company, 1972); Ray H. Mattison's *Devils Tower National Monument—A History* (Devils Tower: Devils Tower Natural History Association, 1973); T. A. Larson's *History of Wyoming,* 2 ed. rev. (Lincoln: University of Nebraska, 1978). A copy of the original handbill advertising the Rogers climb is at Cheyenne at the Wyoming State Archives, Museums and Historical Department in the Devils Tower vertical file. Information on the flag planted on top of the tower by Will Rogers is from the Dick Stone manuscript, in a September 9, 1934 interview with Mr. and Mrs. Truman Fox. See also Truman Fox's "First Flag on Devils Tower" (Cheyenne: Wyoming State Archives, Museums and Historical Department, WPA File 62). Newspaper clippings from the *Sundance Reform,* 6 July 1893 provided some statistical information. I am indebted to Shirley Rathbun, Crook County resident, for Ripley family history she provided in a personal interview conducted in Casper, Wyoming, on January 8, 1982. Climbing information was based on material in Chris Jones's *Climbing in North America* (Berkeley: University of California, 1976); Steve Roper and Allen Steck's *Fifty Classic Climbs of North America* (San Francisco: Sierra Club, 1979); Terry Rypkema and Curt Haire's *A Climber's Guide to Devils Tower* (Devils Tower: n.p.). See also Steve Gardiner and Dick Guilmette's *Devils Tower National Monument: A Climber's Guide* (Seattle: The Mountaineers, 1986). Newspaper accounts include an article in the *Sundance Times*, 11 July 1937. Quoted sections from the writings of Lawrence Coveney are taken from his article "Ascent of Devils Tower," *Appalachia* (1937). Quoted sections from the writings of William P. House are taken from his article "Devils Tower," *American Alpine Journal* (1938). See also Newel Joyner's "Devils Tower," *Appalachia 20* (December, 1934) and Harrison Butterworth's "Second Ascent of Devils Tower, Wyoming," *Appalachia* (1938).

Media Events

For more than a century images of Devils Tower have circled the globe: in paintings and photographs; on calendars, postcards and publicity folders; and, since the 1970s, by way of television and movie screens.

Perhaps the first to photograph it was an unknown photographer with the Newton-Jenney expedition of 1875. St. Louis photographer Robert Benecke somehow obtained the collection of forty-odd stereopticon views which included three of Devils Tower— still known then as Bear Lodge—and one of the Missouri Buttes. Exhibited at the St. Louis Fair in 1876, they received first prize for the best photographic exhibit.

And in 1892 photographer William Henry Jackson (then forty-nine years old) and artist Thomas Moran (then fifty-five), close friends whose photographs and paintings of the Yellowstone country twenty-two years earlier contributed greatly to designation of that first national park, returned to Wyoming. State officials had invited them to prepare something "new and startling" for Wyoming's contribution to the World Columbian Exposition to be held in Chicago the following year.

Jackson and Moran, along with Jackson's assistant named Millett, planned a return trip to Yellowstone and the Tetons by way of Gillette and the Big Horn Mountains. The unusual circumstances of their journey to Devils Tower led to Moran's single, published magazine article.

97

In 1892 Wyoming state officials invited William H. Jackson and artist Thomas Moran to the state to prepare an exhibit for the World Columbian Exposition. This self-portrait of Jackson and his assistant, Millett, indicates how much equipment was still necessary for field photography before the turn of the century. *(Photo by William H. Jackson, courtesy of Colorado Historical Society)*

Dressed for western field work, Thomas Moran often rode horseback and carried his ever-present sketch book. *(Jefferson National Expansion/ National Park Service)*

The trio rented the only available team and wagon in Gillette, and, assured they ''just couldn't miss it,'' set out for Devils Tower the second week in June. They planned to stop at local ranches for meals, taking only Jackson's camera and equipment, Moran's sketching materials and watercolor tubes and a few blankets.

Temporarily lost because of branching roadways and wandering cattle trails, they arrived, hungry, at the 101 Ranch about two in the afternoon. The foreman informed them he didn't keep a roadhouse. Stopping farther ahead to ask the way, they received a set of unclear directions. Beyond some deserted cabins, the road branched out. Taking the most traveled, they caught sight of Devils Tower rising against the sky.

All the while dark purplish storm clouds were piling up in the west. Wyoming's western un-hospitality was nothing compared to the storm the men endured.

A sudden, severe hail storm broke overhead. They could see only a few feet in front of them. All three wore light felt hats and summer clothing. Any tarps which might have afforded protection were tightly packed and strapped down to protect Jackson's camera, the chemicals and glass photographic plates.

The horses at first refused to move, then suddenly lunged and almost upset the wagon. By now the men's hands were bruised from the large hail stones. Their heads stung from blows and showed some lumps. As the hail slacked off, the wind came up and a drenching rain fell. Finally the storm spent itself and the skies lightened, and the men discovered another obstacle.

"Do you know what gumbo is?" wrote Moran in *Century Magazine.* " . . .the clay of northern Wyoming. When wet it is the stickiest, most Indian-rubber-like mud that exists on earth." They walked alongside the wagon to relieve the horses of the extra weight, boots sinking into several inches of mud. They were forced to make frequent stops to scrape their boots and the wagon wheels. By now it was nearly dark. They made their way to a clump of pines on a hillside, pleasantly surprised to find it had been the camp of a herder, whose dry pine-bough beds were still there. Finding some dry matches, they made a fire, dried out their clothing and blankets and spent the night.

The next morning they backtracked, unloading the wagon to cross the worst of the gumbo. They entered a canyon, again uncertain as to which of several roads to take, as roadways stretched out on both sides of the Belle Fourche River. They noticed smoke rising in the distance and approached a cabin where they were made welcome, grateful for their first food and water in thirty-eight hours.

They were directed to cross over the next high ridge and ford the river. "And such a descent we made," Moran wrote. "A narrow trail over a series of sandstone terraces so steep and rocky that I never expected to see our wagon at the bottom . . . Knowing that we were at last on the right road for Devils Tower . . .

This pencil sketch by Thomas Moran, entitled *Hail Storm on Cabin Creek on the Way to Devils Tower*, was typical of the quick blocking out of a composition so he could return to it at a later time, back in his studio. *(National Museum of American Art, Smithsonian Institution, Gift of Dr. William Henry Holmes)*

we almost forgot the sufferings of the previous day.''

"The scenery along the road to the tower was fine," he noted, " . . .enclosing a fertile valley studded with houses and fields of prosperous ranches and farms.'' They had been directed to go to Johnson's (also called Johnston's) and assumed it was a hotel and eating place.

But the Johnsons were wealthy English ranchers, whose frame house was lavishly furnished, even having a grand piano. Through a large window they could see Devils Tower, about twelve miles in the distance. Moran, Jackson and Millett spent the night there.

Moran, W. H. Jackson and his assistant spent the night as a guest of the Johnsons (or Johnston's), wealthy English ranchers who lived about twelve miles from Devils Tower. Moran painted this wash of the view from Johnston's. Devils Tower was visible from one of their large picture windows. *(National Museum of American Art, Smithsonian Institution, gift of the estate of John Holme Maghee)*

This field sketch, *The Rising Storm Cloud*, bears Thomas Moran's notations for further development. He noted "clear sky" and "arroyo." The horse-drawn wagon on the right is similar to the one sketched in "Hail Storm on the Way to Cabin Creek," also sketched on location in Wyoming. *(Jefferson National Expansion/National Park Service)*

This pencil sketch of the tower by Thomas Moran demonstratres Moran's style of blocking out his compositions. *(Jefferson National Expansion/National Park Service)*

Before breakfast the next morning, Johnson had his men run in the horse herd, more than a hundred head, to show the visitors. While at Johnson's, Moran made several sketches.

About noon of that day they reached Devils Tower, together choosing the sites for photographing and sketching. Among Jackson's illustrations resulting from this trip were a half dozen photographs, several showing the tower rising above the winding river. Moran's drawings, perhaps developed from notes and field sketches completed after he returned to his studio, accompanied the article published in *Century Magazine*. They included "The Gathering Storm Cloud," "The Hail Storm," "Devils Tower on the Belle Fourche" and "Devils Tower from Johnson's."

The same summer that Moran and Jackson's Wyoming display was exhibited at the Chicago Exposition commemorating the four-hundredth anniversary of Columbus's discovery of America, the Rogers-Ripley ladder climb drew regional attention to the state's unique rock tower.

Thirteen years later, in 1906, Devils Tower became the first of a number of national monuments. But little development took place until the late 1920s and early 1930s.

As late as 1916 visitors had to walk over a mile and a half, following a partially washed-out trail over log-filled gullies to reach the spring by the picnic area. At several Fourth of July celebrations, Wyomingites circulated petitions demanding improvements. Pressure continued until a bridge over the Belle Fourche River was constructed in 1928.

As state highways were improved during the early 1930s, the tower became more accessible and received wider newspaper and magazine publicity.

Tales of a great cavern beneath Devils Tower with an underground lake, its shores strewn with gold, circulated for a number of years. The *Sundance Times* on April 5, 1934, reported in a non-bylined article the following story, headlined "Legend of Untold Wealth in Gold and Lake of Crystal Water Beneath Devils Tower."

Six of William H. Jackson's photographs of Devils Tower were among work exhibited with the Wyoming contribution to the World Columbian Exposition held in Chicago in 1893. *(Photo by William H. Jackson, courtesy of Colorado Historical Society)*

Despite the Great Depression, the decade of the 1930s was one of Park Service expansion. Civilian Conservation Corps personnel constructed buildings and laid out trails and campgrounds. *(Wyoming State Archives, Museums and Historical Department)*

The article recounts the story of an unnamed early resident of Wyoming who visited Yankton, South Dakota, in the late 1890s. He took with him a picture of the tower and showed it to several Indians. One became very excited and asked if a passageway had been found at the base.

When informed there was no passageway, the Indian fell silent. Only upon the urging of the others did he continue.

The Indian said that long ago, three of his tribe were hunting near the tower. While roaming through the rocks they discovered a passageway which led directly under it.

With pitch pine-knot torches they explored the passage for about eight hundred yards. Torchlight reflected off the cavern walls, and they discovered many bones—possibly human bones. Deeper into the cave was a lake of clear water, probably seventy-five feet long by fifty feet wide. All around the lake were more bones, the Indian said, and "gold in great quantities." But they took no gold, leaving the cavern and closing the entrance so that no one else would discover it.

In 1910, 1911 and again in 1913, Wyoming Congressman Frank Mondell introduced bills for providing an appropriation to build an iron stairway from the foot of the tower to the summit. Each was referred to the Committee on Appropriation, but all three bills died in committee. Later suggestions that the National Park Service construct a steel ladder or elevator were coldly received, the opinion of Custodian Newell Joyner in 1934 being that "much of the romance and glamor of the tower would be lost by such a travesty . . ."

Others eyed the tower for more commercial reasons. In a May 4, 1934, article, the *Kemmerer Gazette* noted that if the tower were crushed into gravel, "a continuous road with gravel four inches deep encircling the earth nine times at the equator" could be built. Several months later another *Gazette* article estimated the weight of Devils Tower to be 400 million tons.

A short article in the *Sheridan Press,* February 26, 1933, noted that Devils Tower was the subject of investigation by "expert granite men" from Vermont. In the tower itself and tributary to it, the article suggested "an inexhaustible supply of granite" which "equals in quality the millions of dollars worth of granite that has been taken from the quarries of Vermont and sent to nearly every quarter of the globe."

The first full-time custodian of the tower was appointed in 1930. During the following decade, extensive improvements were made at Devils Tower, much of it by workers with the Civilian Conservation Corps stationed there between 1933 and 1941.

Growing numbers of tourists appreciated the improved roads, footpaths, picnic grounds and the new museum and visitor center. Employee residences were also constructed, as well as new electrical and water systems. Between 1931 and 1941 the number of visitors almost tripled, from 11,000 to 32,951 annually.

And, as if to make up for a number of ordinary seasons, in

October of 1941 an event took place at Devils Tower which has perhaps never been equaled for on-the-spot excitement. Shoving even Hitler and the World Series scores aside was the news that a young, twenty-nine-year-old daredevil had safely parachuted —without Park Service permission—onto the country's first national monument. Even more entertaining would be the six-day saga of attempts to rescue "Devils Tower George" which hit headlines from Honolulu to London.

About daylight on October 1, George Hopkins and young South Dakota pilot Joe Quinn left Rapid City in a two-passenger plane. The weather was clear but cold, with a stiff ground wind of about thirty-five miles an hour. According to plans worked out ahead of time, Hopkins knew he must guide his parachute to land within a certain area to avoid a huge boulder fused into the tower top. Aiming for that small plot, he left the plane about twelve hundred feet above the rock shaft and fifteen hundred feet south of it.

Fearing he would overshoot, Hopkins partially collapsed his chute to check his drift. Descending even more rapidly, he put one foot forward to keep from overshooting the raised rock and skinned his ankle, landing tight against one side of the boulder with his chute on the other side. Elated with success, Hopkins collapsed his parachute and weighted it down with rocks.

Quinn returned to the hayfield thirty minutes away where they had left Hopkins' odd assortment of down-climbing gear: a sledge hammer, a Ford axle sharpened on one end, a hayloft pulley and two strands of rope.

Stationed below were Hopkins' backers, Earl Brockelsby and his wife of Rapid City. Newsreel photographers completed their filming and Robert Dean, radio station KOTA owner, returned to Rapid City to release a wire service story that Brockelsby had bet Hopkins fifty dollars that Hopkins could not land on top of Devils Tower.

Not released was the full story. George Hopkins had chosen Rapid City as the site for his attempt to set a new world's record (then set at thirty) for the most consecutive parachute jumps in one day. The Chamber of Commerce had agreed to sponsor an

In 1941, George Hopkins became the only man to reach the top of Devils Tower by parachute. Promoters released a wire-service story that Hopkins had parachuted to the top of the National Monument to win a $50 bet. At the time he held a number of impressive U.S. records: the most parachute jumps (2,347), the record for jumping from the greatest height (26,400 feet), and the world's record for the longest delayed jump (20,800 feet). *(Wyoming State Archives, Museums, and Historical Department)*

Hopkins used only one parachute for the jump, a 1929 Irvin seat pack with a 24 foot canopy of pongee silk. He reasoned that even if the lines fouled, it would be easier to handle one parachute than to manipulate lines of an additional emergency parachute. *(courtesy Earl Brockelsby collection)*

Pilot Joe Quinn circled away from the tower after the Hopkins jump. A brisk wind was blowing the morning of the parachute jump. Quinn compared air currents around the top of Devils Tower with waves in a fast-moving stream when water strikes an obstacle jutting up from a riverbed. Wind currents battered his 65 horsepower Aeronca Chief like swift water pounding at a light canoe. *(courtesy Earl Brockelsby collection)*

air show featuring Hopkins, with proceeds to be donated to hospital construction. Parachuting to the top of Devils Tower and staying there for an hour or two seemed the perfect stunt to publicize the show.

Descent plans, also worked out beforehand on paper, called for Hopkins to hammer the sharpened axle into the rock, attach the hundred foot rope to the axle and through the pulley, then add the thousand foot length. If he ran out of rope near the bottom, he thought he could scramble for ledges and toe holds.

After about an hour, Quinn returned to drop the climbing equipment and ropes. But when the rope bundle landed, it bounced off, snagging about fifty feet down on some bushes growing out of the tower sides. Hopkins waved to signal for another rope and

Earl Brockelsby's problems began. Not only did he have to calm Custodian Newell Joyner, he had to locate another pilot since Quinn flew back to Rapid City and couldn't be reached.

Later that afternoon Clyde Ice, veteran Spearfish, South Dakota, pilot flew in, throwing a second, loosely-coiled rope from his plane. Within a few minutes Hopkins tossed to the ground a message tied to a rock informing Brockelsby the rope was so tangled he would have to spend the night on the tower.

Only an hour of daylight remained. Pilot Ice flew out for supplies, returning to drop food, blankets, a tarpaulin and a note from Brockelsby saying, ''We'll get you off tomorrow.'' Within an hour a storm front closed in, isolating the top of the monument. Hopkins rolled into a ball of blankets, shivering in the rain and sleet.

About daylight he ate some sandwiches. When the morning sunlight penetrated the fog, he dropped a note down saying he thought he could parachute to the ground. He signed it ''Devils Tower George.''

Meanwhile, news of the lone man stranded on his ''sky island'' had spread. By late afternoon of the second day over a thousand sightseers, photographers, press and radio correspondents had flocked to the scene.

Feature writers researching Hopkins' background learned that his fascination with planes and parachutes began when barnstormers landed in a field near his boyhood Oregon home. As a young man he toured with air shows as a wing walker and trick parachutist. Hopkins had been a stunt pilot, crashing planes and parachuting from flaming aircraft for the movies.

But Park Service officials in Washington ruled out his parachuting off Devils Tower. Instead they were sending park ranger Ernest K. Field and climbing guide Warren Gorrell from Colorado with alpine climbing rescue equipment.

Earl Brockelsby scribbled a note to tell Hopkins that the parachute jump had been vetoed as Clyde Ice removed the doors of his airplane to prepare for another food drop. Although experienced at evacuation of flood and forest fire victims and a veteran

George Hopkins had ample time to explore the tower top during his six-day sojourn. News of his plight pushed war news and World Series scores aside. Reporters and thousands of spectators flocked to the area. *(courtesy Earl Brockelsby collection)*

of mercy flights to hospitals, for this mission Ice developed a new technique. Because of sudden updrafts around the tower that battered his small, sixty-five horsepower plane, Ice cut the motor, gliding in about six feet above the monument's top. Then, as he signaled his partner to shove out the packages, he restarted the motor.

Hopkins received food packets, water containers, wool blankets, a megaphone and the surprise gift of a medium rare T-bone steak. Despite straw packing, most of the containers split. He shared snacks with birds and chipmunks. Thanks to the bearskin-lined flying suit Ice also dropped, Hopkins' second night was warmer. His third day passed uneventfully, but not so on the ground.

Crowds increased. An amateur radio club established communications between the tower base and an airstrip three miles east. Field and Gorrell arrived before daylight and began climbing about noon.

After examining the Wiessner route and deciding the long crack would be too difficult, they looked at the Durrance approach. Ascending as high as the top of the leaning column, the two decided the long crack that lay ahead was also tough. Both climbers tried a number of ways to ascend this pitch—frontwards, backwards, sideways.

Newell Joyner's office phone rang steadily and telegrams poured in. One suggested that the sheriff of Los Angeles "lasso the stranded parachutist." Another advised dropping whiskey, having Hopkins drink it and fall over the edge because "the Lord takes care of drunken people." Someone proposed firing a rope up by cannon. Many telegrams also expressed concern for Hopkins' safety.

He passed time nibbling candy bars and fried chicken a ranch wife fixed for him when she heard he had eaten sardines and Ritz crackers for breakfast.

Several hours into their climb, one of the two rescuers slipped. Saved from injury by the ropes, they returned to the ground. Meanwhile, Jack Durrance had wired Joyner that he would leave Dartmouth College in New Hampshire immediately to assist in the rescue. With him would be several other experienced climbers.

Later that same afternoon Earl Brockelsby was served a surprise along with coffee in Joyner's office. The Goodyear Blimp "Reliance" was reportedly coming to lift Hopkins off Devils Tower with a special pickup basket, arrangements courtesy of an Omaha, Nebraska, newspaper.[1]

Hopkins spent a long night dozing, trying to keep warm. When ice stiffened his coverall cuffs, he stood and exercised, chainsmoking cigarettes.

---

[1]Sources differ on the matter of the blimp. Archives of the Goodyear Tire and Rubber Company show that the "Reliance" was involved in a rescue mission near Akron, Ohio, during the first week in October, 1941.

Day four dawned cold, with high winds. A new storm center was brewing over the Black Hills, with parts of the Dakotas reporting rain mixed with snow. By now area hotels and motels were full. Grocery store shelves were almost bare, and the few phone lines were tied up by newsmen calling in their stories long distance.

Most major American newspapers had already featured the tale of Devils Tower George in print and cartoons. *Time* and *Newsweek* magazines ran items, playing up anecdotes.

Several *Good Housekeeping* magazines, fuel oil and a load of coal from the Sheridan Coal Company were brought to the airstrip. A prefabricated hut similar to a doghouse was sent from a nearby lumberyard, but the pre-cut sections were too large to fit into Ice's cockpit.

Other planes buzzed like mosquitoes around the tower. One rancher collected damages when airplane propeller blasts scattered his haystacks. Another spent the day rounding up horses spooked by low-flying planes. Finally Joyner grounded all aircraft just before Field and Gorrell again climbed.

Attempting to make Durrance's rescue job easier, Field and Gorrell obtained a thirty-foot extension ladder. Aided by a ground crew and several long ropes, they maneuvered the ladder to the top of the leaning column. They extended it to its full length and secured it to the rock wall. By late afternoon, the first, most difficult pitch was scalable.

The following day Park Service mechanic Frank Heppler brought in some heavy iron spikes to be used in the upper portion of the crack which was too wide for regular pitons. Higher up, some two-by-fours were pounded in.

By now, Durrance should have phoned from Cheyenne, but there was still no word.

That afternoon Joyner received another offer of assistance from Paul Petzoldt of Jackson. An experienced climbing instructor and professional alpinist, Petzoldt had climbed in the Himalayas and in Wyoming's Tetons. Petzoldt and park ranger Harold Rapp set out for the all-night drive despite blizzard warnings.

Then Joyner received a telegram that the Durrance party was

enroute to Denver by train. Storms in the midwest had cancelled all westbound flights out of Chicago.

By Sunday morning, October 5, temperatures had dropped and a freezing mist was falling.

"Do you need anything? A change of clothes?" Joyner called up to Hopkins through a megaphone.

"No, I'm not going anywhere today," answered Hopkins, pausing between words because of echoes.

About noon Petzoldt and Rapp pulled in, their car mounded with snow. Field and Gorrell joined them, having been forced down from another attempt by ice glazing the tower sides. With the weather threatening, tempers exploded. The climbers insisted on going for Hopkins. Blimp promoters in the crowd argued for holding off.

About midnight a caravan of police and highway patrol cars with sirens on and lights flashing escorted Durrance's borrowed car in.

The climb was set for daylight.

That night there was talk that Hopkins might have to be brought down as dead weight, if he were weak or disoriented due to exposure.

Monday morning at 7:30 they began, Durrance leading, followed by Petzoldt and the others. Gusts of wind whipped at the men. The tower sides were spotted with ice and packed snow, but a major storm had not moved in.

As Durrance himself later described it in an article in *Appalachia*: "Clouds hung over the tower as we started . . . and thin ice coated the rock. Later it snowed, so thank God for the ladder! Besides the ladder, every conceivable piton was used, as well as 2 × 4 stakes which were driven into the crack to stand on . . . All this aid was necessitated not only by our very poor physical condition . . . but also by the weather and the cold, slippery rock."

As Field commented in *Trail and Timberline*: "Durrance was soon standing on the topmost rung of the ladder, becoming reacquainted with the thirty feet remaining of the sixty foot pitch.

Warren Gorrell and I gaped in awe and admiration. Jack accomplished the thirty feet in slightly over two hours. Durrance climbed facing the wall, utilizing friction holds on the sloping column faces, and jamming his right foot into the larger crack when width permitted . . . the driving of wooden pegs and pitons while hanging on a vertical pitch with friction holds calls for perfect skill and balance in large measures. Durrance did a marvelous piece of work.''

All eight climbers, roped together by 125 feet of rope, went up. In crossing to a shelf about 150 feet below the tower top, each had to make the four-foot jump from one sloping ledge to another over a five-hundred-foot drop.[2]

After eight hours of climbing, Durrance came into Hopkins' view.

''I heard the climbers making their way slowly up the sides,'' Hopkins recalled in Dale M. Titler's book, *Wings of Adventure.* ''I wasn't able to see them until they were within seventy-five feet of me . . . Durrance stopped several feet below me and waited, out of reach. He talked with me and I knew he was looking me over carefully, trying to decide whether I was going to lose my head at the thought of being rescued. When he was satisfied I was completely rational, he came over the top.

''That was the greatest moment! I knew for the first time I was really safe! The others followed until the largest assembly of men—nine in all—were gathered on top of Devils Tower.

''Daylight was going fast. While the climbers rested and ate lunch, I told them I could go down as one of their party if they'd just show me what to do. They demonstrated the rappel . . . Because of his strength and experience in teaching beginners, Paul Petzoldt was selected to belay me down. He tied a stout rope around me in case of a slip, and we started down at 4:45 P.M. Progress was slow because he took every precaution. He snubbed the descent rope around a rock or piton, and his own

---

[2]Durrance brought with him from Dartmouth a friend named Merril McLane, according to Field's article. Other climbers joining them in Denver were Henry Coulter and Chappell Cranmer.

Climbers from several states came to assist in George Hopkins' rescue: (not identified in order) Paul Petzoldt, standing at center, and Harold Rapp from Jackson Hole, Wyoming; Jack Durrance and Merrill McClane from New Hampshire; Ernest Field, Warren Gorrell, Chappell Cranmer and Harry Coulter from Colorado. *(courtesy Earl Brockelsby collection)*

body, then paid it out slowly. We repeated this in short belays all the way down.''

Dusk came just before six. Radio and sound trucks with floodlights were pulled in close to light up the tower base, but the last two hundred feet were made in total darkness. About 9:30, the last of the climbers stepped into the glare of car headlights, and a loud roar from the crowd.

Earl Brockelsby gripped George Hopkins' hands.

A reporter thrust a microphone toward the exhausted, windburned Hopkins, asking at what point during his six-day ordeal was he the most frightened.

''Never was,'' answered George. ''But I'd rather climb back

up than face that crowd. Boy, I'll never grow whiskers. This six-day beard is terrible."

Newell Joyner's statement confirmed that "the National Park Service doesn't welcome this kind of publicity, but we are most grateful that we were able to get George safely to the ground," and he added that he would "take steps to prevent repetition of this sort of thing."

Later at a local clinic, Hopkins was declared in excellent condition, weighing 124 pounds, a gain of one pound for each of the six days he spent aloft.

"I owe my life to the climbers who rescued me and to the flyers who dropped me food and clothing," he said. "This was not exhibition jumping. It was partly to let people know just what a person can do with a parachute if he really knows one."

But his near-perfect landing on Devils Tower hadn't impressed the public nearly so much as the fact that he couldn't get down.

Enjoying his moments in the sun, Hopkins spoke in several South Dakota theaters following newsreel screenings of his jump and rescue. Later in the month he flew to New York City to appear on a nationwide radio show and visited in Washington with Wyoming Senator Joseph C. O'Mahoney. He also met there with a group of scientists to discuss plant and animal life on the tower top and described in detail some "curious crystals" he discovered.[3]

---

[3]As planned, a week after his rescue from Devils Tower, George Hopkins attempted a new jump record at the Rapid City air show. On his third jump his parachute strung out, causing him to land hard on the concrete runway. Doctors insisted he quit, but he made ten more jumps before giving up, bruised and exhausted. Ironically, he was to make more than thirty jumps in a day on several occasions in the course of his work. After the bombing of Pearl Harbor, he enlisted in the army and trained paratroopers at Ft. Benning, Georgia. Later he served with the Office of Strategic Services, developing new methods of dropping men and equipment behind enemy lines. He flew again at air shows and for the Mexican Federal Police. In 1958, he flew for the last time. He worked for a number of years with a high-rise construction firm. George Hopkins died in 1977 in Norwalk, California.

Newsmen in the Denver office of United Press named the Hopkins episode the Rocky Mountain News Story of the Year. They called it a "natural" as a news story, possessing all the necessary qualities—suspense, uniqueness, action and a touch of humor.

Though much less spectacular than the Hopkins rescue, another project drew to a close in the winter of 1942. New York artist Perry Wilson completed a large painting of Devils Tower to be used as the background for a diorama displayed there at the American Museum of Natural History. Still displayed in the North American Mammal Hall, the diorama features a group of mule deer browsing among native Wyoming plants.

In 1954, an elderly Oklahoma native proposed a religious statue for the top of Devils Tower, though it apparently attracted little support.

Annoyed at all the place names involving "devil," Richard Colbert Mason of Tulsa visualized a statue of Christ, similar to the Christ of the Andes statue on the Chile-Argentina border. The proposed statue would be constructed of white porcelain brick on a structural frame; the hands and feet would be pink porcelain brick. Around the head would be a halo of gold-plated aluminum and at the feet of the 240-foot statue, twenty-foot-high neon letters would spell out "Peace on Earth—Good Will to Men" and "U.S.A." Mason believed a small turbine installed in the Belle Fourche River could provide power to light up the statue, which would also act as an airplane beacon.

"That Devils Tower has been sitting out there in the Black Hills for a million years and nobody paid any attention to it," he told *Tulsa World* reporters. He added that that statue "would be the best answer in the world to communism, too." He hoped to enlist a committee of evangelists, bankers, businessmen and attorneys in his non-profit venture.

A more publicized event of the 1950s was the Golden Anniversary, celebrated July 14–22, 1956. Mountaineer's Week featured massed climbing assaults to demonstrate to the nearly fifteen

IN PERSON!

THE SIX-DAY PARACHUTE HERMIT OF

DEVIL'S TOWER

GEORGE HOPKINS

See and Hear the most Fantastic Parachute Jumper in Aviation History!

FRIDAY & SATURDAY ONLY

PARAMOUNT

Hopkins spoke in several theaters following newsreel showings of his jump and rescue. He was interviewed on a New York radio show and flew on to Washington to meet with Wyoming's Congressional delegation and to discuss plant and animal life on the tower top with a group of scientists. *(courtesy Earl Brockelsby collection)*

thousand visitors that climbing is a safe sport for individuals trained in the skills of climbing. All climbers, in order to participate, had to be certified by letter as competent.

Over eighty ascents were made and some new routes pioneered by climbers from more than a dozen states, as well as teams from France, Switzerland, Canada, and the U.S. Army. Also featured were simulated rescue operations, demonstrating how to rescue injured or incapacitated climbers.

Four Casper, Wyoming, men—Walt Bailey, Gary Cole, Dud McReynolds and David Sturdevant—received permission to spend the night on top of the tower. The fire they built to grill steaks was visible for miles. Later in the evening, rain fell and army helicopters dropped them ponchos for shelter.

During the fifties and sixties interest in climbing and outdoor activities increased. Between 1963 and 1973 the total number of climbers to reach the summit of Devils Tower increased three hundred percent, from one thousand to three thousand. By 1975, four thousand climbers had made it, over a number of different routes.

In mid-May 1976, Columbia/EMI film crews came to Wyoming for twelve days location filming of writer-director Steven Spielberg's motion picture, *Close Encounters of the Third Kind*, its theme—contact with extra-terrestrial beings. Night scenes with helicopter pursuits were filmed, for which the film company posted a $100,000 bond in the event that any damages occurred. Several hundred Wyoming people played the parts of extras in a crowd of "terrified residents" who were, according to the script, being evacuated because of what officials said was a dangerous chemical spill resulting from derailment of some tank cars.

More than one hundred million people viewed *Close Encounters* in its first, 1977 version, according to movie ads. Haunted by an image of a tall tower, Roy Neary (Richard Dreyfuss) becomes obsessed with building replicas of it in shaving cream, mashed potatoes and mud. Artist Jillian Guilar (Melinda Dillon) whose young son, Barry (Cary Guffey), disappears under mysterious circumstances, is compelled to paint pictures of a tall, rocky spire, over and over. With a group of other earthlings, Roy and Jillian are inevitably drawn to Devils Tower and closer contact with aliens after seeing a TV news story about the chemical spill, a story manufactured to cover up the real one. Teri Garr plays Dreyfuss's wife. The late film director Francois Truffaut portrays a sympathetic scientist.

A hit with reviewers as well as the public, the film was called "the most important film of our time" by science fiction writer Ray Bradbury and "one of the most spectacular movies ever made" by critic Rex Reed. According to a Variety magazine poll, in January 1980, *Close Encounters of the Third Kind* ranked ninth of the top ten moneymaking movies of all time, at that writing.

Its release that year in England, Ireland and Scotland prompted many letters and phone calls to the monument headquarters asking for more information, according to former Superintendent Homer Robinson. And that same summer, in an unprecedented move, the film was revised. A few portions were cut, some outtakes inserted and new footage added to create *The Special Edition of Close Encounters of the Third Kind*. Critics again responded enthusiastically. Several suggested that the most effective addition was the new ending, showing what Roy Neary sees as he enters the huge, cathedral-like spacecraft filled with limitless light and the wonders of a new, alien technology.

While the movie was playing in theaters and on television, in April of 1979, George Willig, a "media hero" known for his 1977 climb of the World Trade Center in New York City, and a partner, Steve Matous, climbed Devils Tower for ABC television's "Wide World of Sports." Nine cameras were required in order that armchair viewers could share Willig's roped, free climb, made without the use of pitons. In addition, Willig wore a wireless microphone so viewers could hear his comments as he struggled upward.

While both Willig's climb and the movie, *Close Encounters,* probably contributed to a jump in attendance over a period of several years, the impact of the coal boom in nearby Campbell

County also contributed, as did ever-increasing numbers of climbers, according to former Superintendent Robinson. In 1981 alone, 3,302 people attempted to climb Devils Tower, but fewer than half—1,613—reached the top.

The Spielberg movie attracted others to the area for still different reasons. Searching for UFOs and salvation in the mid-seventies, a middle-aged couple known as Herff and Bonnie (also called The Two, Bo and Peep, Winnie and Poo, Chip and Dale) led a group of some two dozen followers out of Los Angeles looking for a spacecraft to take them to a new kingdom. According to one report, the group exceeds a thousand. Cult members prefer to stay to themselves, searching out "high strangeness" in remote locations with high rates of UFO sightings. Followers of Herff and Bonnie have been noted by observers, in the parking lot across from the visitor's center at the base of Devils Tower.

On September 24, 1981, Devils Tower celebrated its Diamond Jubilee—its seventy-fifth birthday as a national monument—with a potluck dinner provided by the Hulett, Wyoming, Future Homemakers of America and the Devils Tower Natural History Association, an organization which raises funds to help pay for programs, displays and other extras not provided by the Park Service. Following the meal, several hundred visitors adjourned to the campfire and outdoor amphitheater for a historical slide presentation and a series of speakers. Among the speakers was Lorraine Mintzmeyer, Rocky Mountain Regional Director of the National Park Service.

"If the national parks are big jewels (in the national park system), then the national monuments are small gems," she told the crowd. She added that places such as Devils Tower are also educational laboratories.

A careful look at the monument grounds shows nature at work. The chain of rock to soil to forest can be seen here. Bright yellow lichen and moss cling to rocks along the mile-long trail that rings the tower base. Small shelves and fissures fill with dust. Grass sprouts. Flowers follow—Queen Anne's Lace, wild roses. Sagebrush, currants, chokecherries and low shrubs take root. Pines and aspens only inches high lean into checkerboards of sunlight below the parent trees. Here and there, porcupines have stripped wide bands of bark from trees, to reach sweet inner layers. Burr oak trees flourish, but grow nowhere else in Wyoming. Many western songbirds nest here.

All animals on the grounds are protected. They seem to know it. Does and fawns clatter up and down the pavement. In June, the summer's young, fuzzy prairie dogs first come above ground. There are beavers, raccoons, badgers, squirrels, chipmunks, and, less appreciated, rattlesnakes. Turkey vultures flap into crowns of tall ponderosas near the museum.

On some mornings, flocks of wild turkeys—hens, toms and their offspring—drift through the silver-green grass of an open meadow. Tourists photograph them, rest, hike the trail, picnic. Travelers from all over the world have come here to enjoy the outdoors and see the unique tower.

To others, Devils Tower will always be a holy place, predating Christianity.

"A powerful medicine place, where people go to seek visions . . . a lot like Bear Butte in South Dakota," Sioux spokesman Milo Yellow Hair described Devils Tower in an Associated Press story. In late September 1981, a group of about sixty Sioux, among them Hunkpapa, Oglala and others who had previously camped at Bear Butte State Park in South Dakota, gathered at Devils Tower for religious ceremonies. They chose to regroup there, Yellow Hair said, because of the rock tower's special significance.

"This is a religious campaign," he added. "We're going to use it as a base camp for operations to bring in Indians to talk about the 1868 treaty . . ." After several days, the group moved from the public campground to another camp close by for privacy, because they planned a special pipe ceremony with members of the Cheyenne tribe.

At dawn on October 3, several shots were fired near the camp, one hitting a fifty-five-gallon oil drum. No one was injured. Three Hulett men were taken into custody and one was eventually placed on probation and fined.

A few days later a *Denver Post* reporter and photographer were turned away from the campsite, and told "no talk, no pictures. We don't take pictures of your churches." This Sioux camp was not destined to become a media event.

Other Sioux camps in the Black Hills had also been established earlier, among them the Yellow Thunder Camp twelve miles southwest of Rapid City, South Dakota, set up in April of that year. At this writing the Yellow Thunder camp continues. It has been called part of a "new beginning" in the century-long Indian struggle to reclaim ownership of the Black Hills.

In perhaps the largest award ever made by the court of claims, in July 1980, the Supreme Court in an eight to one decision ordered the federal government to pay $105 million to eight tribes of Sioux as partial compensation for illegal seizure of the Black Hills in 1877.

Accepting money for these lands has been compared by tribal leaders with putting a price tag on the Holy Lands of Palestine or accepting payment of several hundred million dollars for the Vatican. A large number of Sioux who live on eight reservations—six in South Dakota and one each in Montana and Nebraska—want these lands returned, or at least those portions not now under private ownership. Some lawyers who represented the Sioux before the Supreme Court have been quoted as saying it is unrealistic for Indian people to expect to regain the land; others suggest that when payment of the money is made, it could be used to purchase land within and adjoining the Sioux reservation where farms and ranches might be established.

Meanwhile, the money, excepting the $10.5 million paid in legal fees, remains in trust funds held by the Department of the Interior.

Vine Deloria, Jr., a Standing Rock Sioux, author, lawyer, and former director of the National Congress of American Indians, wrote in a *Denver Post* article on July 27, 1980, that Congress must first appropriate the money and approve the manner in which the Indian people want to spend it, following a tribal referendum. If the people decide upon a per capita distribution of the money, tribal rolls must be drawn up, consisting of all descendants of the tribes as they existed in 1877.[4]

In a recently published book, *Sioux Indian Religion* (edited by Raymond J. DeMallie and Douglas Parks), current keeper of the Sacred Pipe, Arval Looking Horse, discussed the Pipe in modern Sioux life and related a story about Devils Tower, brought down through oral tradition. Looking Horse, a Minneconjou Sioux from South Dakota's Cheyenne River Reservation, is the nineteenth generation to serve as Pipe Keeper.

Many years ago, he said, a hole ran through Devils Tower from east to west. The tower resembled a big tipi. A man scouting near there entered the opening. On the north side of the tower he saw the Sacred Pipe. On the south side he saw a sacred bow and arrows. The man chose the bow and arrows and walked out the west side of the tower. From that time on the Cheyennes have had their Sacred Arrows. Later, the Pipe was given to the Sioux.

"This is a sacred place, a sacred hill," Looking Horse said.

People gather as they have for centuries to see the stump-shaped rock that guards the river. To walk in coolness below a canopy of burr oak trees. To find a quiet place in this unquiet world.

---

[4]Delivering an hour-long "Twilight Talk" at the Buffalo Bill Historical Center in Cody, Wyoming, June 29, 1988, entitled "The Continuing Controversy Over the Black Hills Settlement," Vine Deloria, Jr., predicted a "coming together process" in the next several years in regard to development of forums for looking at and discussing issues—including joint-management—though at present he sees "no central definition" of issues involved, due, in part, to "media distortion." "The Black Hills situation presents, in my opinion, an unparalleled opportunity for restoration of the (Great) Plains area, for building a stable, very sensible life for Indians and non-Indians . . . ," he said. Deloria sees settlement not as a measure for this generation of Indians to "get even" with the federal government, ". . . but for two generations down the line, setting up a very good way for Indian people to live in rural areas pretty much in the lifestyle they want."

DEVILS TOWER NATIONAL MONUMENT
ANNUAL VISITS

Year	Visitors	Year	Visitors
1937	28,746	1966	124,994
1938	37,500	1967	117,819
1939	27,003	1968	155,245
1940	31,107	1969	139,397
1941	33,000	1970	147,444
1942	24,222	1971	138,372
1943	5,736	1972	150,810
1944	6,046	1973	153,200
1945	7,315	1974	125,592
1946	35,551	1975	151,564
1947	38,406	1976	169,754
1948	51,676	1977	156,293
1949	57,814	1978	272,617
1950	60,139	1979	227,560
1951	68,846	1980	215,402
1952	88,833	1981	300,308
1953	95,858	1982	270,951
1954	100,919	1983	274,265
1955	93,687	1984	228,095
1956	122,284	1985	224,994
1957	104,724	1986	298,148
1958	115,301	1987	334,502
1959	120,399	1988	347,451
1960	116,961	1989	358,853
1961	114,193	1990	433,303
1962	124,927	1991	459,511
1963	125,409	1992	461,010
1964	109,562	1993	428,933
1965	127,568	1994	457,789

Total (1938-1994)   9,397,908

Works Cited

Details and actual prints of the photographs taken of Devils Tower in 1875 can be found in the previously cited book, *The Black Hills Expedition of 1875*. The Thomas Moran trip to Devils Tower is extracted from his article ''A Journey to Devils Tower in Wyoming,'' *Century Magazine* 25 (November 1893–April 1894). See also Thurman Wilkins' *Thomas Moran: Artist of the Mountains* (Norman: University of Oklahoma, 1969); and Carol Clark's *Thomas Moran: Watercolors of the American West* (Austin: University of Texas, 1980). Information and statistics relating to the years between 1916-1941 can be found in the previously cited *Devils Tower National Monument* by Ray Mattison. Much of the information regarding the George Hopkins incident was assembled from undated scrapbook material borrowed from Earl Brockelsby and Reta Mae Maierhauser of Rapid City, South Dakota. Hopkins' direct quotes are taken from the Dale M. Titler book *Wings of Adventure* (New York: Dodd and Mead, 1972). See also the article by Ernest K. Field, ''The Devils Tower Episode,'' *Trail and Timberline* 276 (1941); and the article by Jack Durrance, ''Emergency Ascent of Devils Tower, Wyoming,'' *Appalachia* (1942). The *Sundance Times* for 8 January 1942 carried information about the Hopkins story being selected ''News Story of the Year.'' The *Casper Times*, 29 October1942, recorded the completion of the diorama at the American Museum of Natural History. The *Casper Star Tribune*, 10 October 1954, contained information about the religious statue proposed for the top of Devils Tower. Information about Mountaineer's Week was assembled from the *Sheridan Press*, 17 July 1956; *Sundance Times*, 19 July 1956; and Orrin H. Bonnie and Lorraine G. Bonnie's *Guide to Wyoming's Mountains and Wilderness Areas* 3d ed. rev. (Chicago: Swallow Press, Inc., 1960). Information on the Wyoming filming of *Close Encounters of the Third Kind* was assembled from interviews with former Superintendent Homer Robinson, at Devils Tower, on July 10, 1980 and July 14, 1981. See also

Casper Star Tribune, 15 March 1980, and Ralph Albi's "Box Office Champs" in *Denver Post Empire Magazine*, 18 May 1980. George Willig's climb was documented in the *Gillette News-Record*, 11 April 1979. Herff and Bonnie's interest in the Devils Tower area is mentioned in Dennis Hanson's article "The Devil's Truth" in *Audubon* 83 (1981). The tower's Diamond Jubilee was featured in the *Casper Star Tribune*, 25 September 1981. Information about the Sioux encampment at Devils Tower was assembled from the following newspapers: *Casper Star Tribune*, 28 September 1981 and 28 October 1981; *Sheridan Press*, 29 September 1981 and 5 October 1981; and *Denver Post*, 11 October 1981. For background on the Supreme Court's decision to award money to the Sioux as compensation for illegal seizure of the Black Hills see Vine Deloria, Jr's. article "Black Hills Dilemma" in the *Denver Post*, 27 July 1980, and also "Sovereignty" in *The Great Sioux Nation*, previously cited. The story told by Arval Looking Horse can be found in the section "The Sacred Pipe in Modern Life" from *Sioux Indian Religion*, edited by Raymond J. DeMallie and Douglas R. Parks (Norman: University of Oklahoma, 1987).

Index

THE AUTHOR, Mary Alice Gunderson, is an "endangered species" native Wyomingite. Born in Sheridan and graduated from the University of Wyoming, she is a former teacher and currently Artist in Residence with the Wyoming Council on the Arts. Since the mid-70s she has taught poetry and short fiction workshops in the Natrona County Schools. She has published on a variety of subjects (health and education issues, Wyoming history, regional personalities, western artists and writers) in *Life and Health*, *Scholastic*, *Empire*, *Horizon*, *South Dakota Review*, and others. She worked for several years in the public relations field. Her short fiction has appeared in *Plainswoman*, *Owen Wister Review*, *Westering* and others. Her poems have appeared in *Poet Lore*, *Voices International* and numerous other literary magazines and in several poetry anthologies including *Poets West: Contemporary Poems from Eleven Western States*, *Point Riders Press Anthology of Great Plains Poetry*, and *Pegasus*.

Among her awards are a research and writing grant from the Wyoming Council for the Humanities; a 1987 Literature Fellowship for fiction from the Wyoming Arts Council; fiction awards from *Plainswoman* Magazine, Wyoming Presswomen and Casper College; and several poetry awards. In 1986 she was artist-in-residence at the Ucross Foundation.

She is a member of Wyoming Presswomen and Western Writers of America. She makes her home in Casper with her husband Ed and son Jim, a college student.

RAYMOND J. DEMALLIE wrote the foreword. DeMallie is the Director of the American Indian Studies Research Institute and professor of anthropology at Indiana University. Author of many articles on Lakota ethnohistory, kinship and social organization, he also edited *The Sixth Grandfather: Black Elk's Teachings Given to John G. Neihardt* and, in 1987, co-edited *Sioux Indian Religion* with Douglas R. Parks.

GISELE ROBINSON is the cover artist and also drew the line illustrations in the book. Mrs. Robinson and her husband Homer, the former superintendent of Devils Tower National Monument, raised their sons near the rugged beauty of the tower and their current home features a spectacular view of the rock formation. She has made a specialty of painting the Black Hills and Devils Tower. Her paintings are in private and public collections in the United States and Europe.

Designed by High Plains Press.
Composed by Crane Typesetting Service, Inc.
in Times Roman
with display lines in Zapf Chancery Demi.
Printed by Thomson-Shore
on Glatfelter Offset.